I0539363

LETTERS TO A DREAMER
VOLUME 1

SHAWN L BAGLEY JR

Prolifik Imagination

For permissions requests, write to the publisher at: Prolifik Imagination (Attn.: Shawn L. Bagley Jr.), P.O. Box 292, Lima, Ohio, 45802 Email: admin@blulightconsulting.com

ISBN: 9798218465599

Published by Prolifik Imagination, P.O. Box 292, Lima, Ohio, 45802

Cover design by Sammie Shigley-Giusti-Laibl

Printed in United States of America

First Edition (Revised: April 2025)

CONTENTS

DEDICATION

*I had a list of people that I wanted to thank in this dedication but I'm afraid that if I did, the list of names would be longer than the book. **Fair warning: the list is still pretty long!***

First, this book is dedicated to my cousin, Chaude'. I miss you more than words can express and I love you beyond forever. Thank you for always protecting me, guiding, and encouraging me. I miss telling jokes under my breath and hearing you laugh out loud because you were the only one who heard it. I believe that those jokes were some of my funniest. I miss our talks and laughing together. Your death shattered me and changed my life in ways I can't begin to describe. This one is for you!

To my grandpa, John *— I love you and miss you. I'd give anything to hear you say **"Right on..."** one more time. Thank you for the lessons over the years. You taught me the power of listening and that there is a lot we can learn from the generations that came before.*

To my Gran *– I love you! I am grateful for you. Thank you for giving me my spiritual foundation and showing me the power of building my relationship with GOD.*

To my mother *– I love you! Thank you for all of the sacrifices you made and all the work that you have done to become the person you* are today. I am proud to call you mine. Thank you for pushing me so hard. I didn't always like it but it made me who I am today. I learned how to be resilient from watching you. I love you beyond forever!

To my uncle Cantrell — thank you for showing me the way. You have been more than an uncle to me. You have been a father-figure and a friend at some of the lowest moments in my life. Before I knew what I wanted from life, you gave me the blueprint and showed me how to be a good man without ever saying a word. I love you beyond comprehension.

To Stasha — the love of my life, my best friend and my future wife, I love you and I am eternally grateful to you and for you. Thank you for being you and thank you for going on this wild ride with me. GOD knew that I would need you. You have encouraged me every step of the way and I know that there had to be a few moments where you thought I was crazy; hell, I did too. We didn't waiver and I couldn't have asked for a better partner in life.

To my babies – Autumn and Nia. I love you so much. You have brought the greatest joy into my life and you are proof that GOD is real and blesses abundantly because you are more than I could have ever asked GOD for and more than I could have ever thought for myself. Don't ever be afraid to shine your light. Know that GOD is with you ALWAYS and in ALL WAYS! I love you!

To my family — I love you all, beyond forever. I know I'm not always around and sometimes it feels like I'm unreachable or too busy for you but that will never be the case. If ever you need me, call me. If you are reading these words, that means that the book exists! Letters to a Dreamer, Volume 1 is here. This is for every sacrifice you made and every dream you deferred. May this collection of letters and any volume produced after, light the way for generations to come.

To the other two members of "The Trifecta" – MJ and Sammie, THANK YOU! Your friendship means the world to me. We've been through a lot together and I appreciate the love, support and encouragement. GOD makes no mistakes and knew that my arms would get tired eventually. Thank you for being my team for tired arms. This is only the beginning!

To Esther Deutsch – Thank you, dear friend! You have been a light in my life. You are a force and I am proud to call you, my friend!

To Ms. G. – Thank you for editing the manuscript for me, I know that rough draft was a little insane! As always, I appreciate your feedback and support over the years! I love you!

Lastly, this book is dedicated to all of my teachers, in both school and life. Thank you.

INTRODUCTION

"Shawn,

In this place you can explore your inner-most feelings – Here you will begin to believe in your abilities and your shortcomings as a young man. Create a world for yourself here and be very careful who you want to enter. You are very special – cultivate your growth here and it will take you to places you never thought existed."

Love,

Uncle Cantrell

I was ten years old the first time I read those words.

They were written in a brown leather journal that my uncle bought me for my birthday.

My journey as a writer started that day.

Recording my reflections in my journal unlocked a part of my mind that I had never explored before.

INTRODUCTION

As a child, I had many thoughts but no way to channel those thoughts or work through my feelings.

Over the past eight years, I have cultivated this collection of letters. I wrote the first letter to myself (it was more like a note) back in 2016.

The purpose of these letters originally was to reflect on my own experiences and to make sense of them in some way.

They were my way of encouraging myself during those dark periods in my life.

Before publishing this collection, I asked a few people to read the manuscript.

A couple of them came back and asked me *"who I was speaking to in the letters?"*

For clarity – I am the *"Dreamer"* that I am speaking to in these letters.

This is not the kind of book that is meant to be read in one sitting or even from cover to cover — although you can read it that way if you wish.

It is not written in any sort of special order. You can open the book to any letter in the collection and start there.

I did not write these with an audience in mind but I hope that you, the reader, can find nuggets of wisdom in this volume.

I wrote these notes and letters to myself in moments where I really needed them.

I hope that you can bring your own experiences to this work and that it resonates with you, no matter where you are in your journey.

Lastly, let's talk about my writing style.

I do not know what made me format the letters this way, but I am glad that I did. This format made the writing process easier for me.

These letters are a collaboration between GOD and myself and originally were never meant to see the light of day.

Whatever your beliefs, these letters focus on three themes – the Human experience, faith, and perseverance.

I have said to friends and family over the years that my podcast was the space where I shared my darkness.

This collection is where I will share my light.

I recently encountered a beautiful quote by the poet Mario Quintana.

"Don't waste your time chasing butterflies. Mend your garden and the butterflies will come."

May this collection be a garden that attracts the most beautiful butterflies, and may it inspire others to create and cultivate gardens of their own.

1

THE PATIENCE THE PROMISE REQUIRES

Dearest Dreamer,

I hate to be the bearer of what some might consider *bad news*, but the elevator to success is broken, so you will have to take the stairs.

The stairs that I'm referring to are reminiscent of the stairs that Langston Hughes wrote about in his poem *Life for Me Ain't Been No Crystal Stair*.

Those stairs will be full of hazards.

There will be bumps and detours, and you will experience significant setbacks.

There will be moments where you want to give up and forget the reason that you set out to pursue your promise in the first place.

You will find yourself in a place where the initial spark that gave birth to a great flame will begin to flicker; the flame withering in the winds of adversity you encounter along your path.

You will be tired.

You will want to give up, and will lose sight of the vision that inspired you to begin your journey.

Your faith will wane in some moments, but I will let you in on a little secret, Dreamer.

It is called a leap of faith because it requires *FAITH*.

Dr. King compared it to taking the first step without seeing the entire staircase.

This journey is a process, and that process is fueled by hard work and effort.

Your effort is sustained by your faith.

The song *A Closer Walk with Thee,* comes to mind as I write this letter and reflect on my own journey.

The journey along the path to your promise will test your faith in ways that you can't even begin to imagine.

You will even come to a place where you are convinced that GOD has forgotten about you.

Convinced that GOD has forsaken you.

Do not allow your mind to run away with these lies.

Don't let fear win.

Success is not a place that you can visit in the physical.

It is not a destination or a future moment in time.

It is subjective.

One thing that remains true for me is that *success is not realized without process.*

Here is another thing to keep in mind; this journey will push you past your limits or at least whatever limitations you believe are holding you back.

You will be tested by people, places, and things.

The pressure of your promise may feel suffocating at times, like the walls of your expectations are closing in on you, slowly killing the flame that fuels you as you push toward your dream.

The journey is perilous and filled with setbacks.

I am not telling you this to scare you.

I am telling you this to prepare you for moments that **WILL** come to pass.

There will be setbacks and there will be victories.

You will experience highs that make every moment of struggle worth it and lows that make you question what the hell made you start on your path in the first place.

Through all of these experiences...*trust the process.*

Trust that every outcome is the result of a process.

Everything has a journey attached to it and that journey has a process and that process has an end result or an outcome.

Always remember that the bigger your vision, the more obstacles you will encounter along your journey.

The promise and/or dream that you are building, requires patience; the kind of patience that some consider virtuous.

The process will require you to continue to believe in a vision that is LOADING…

Don't QUIT!!!

Remember that the bigger your vision, the longer the loading time will be.

Your time will come and when it does, you will be happy that you didn't quit!

The lessons that you will learn on this journey are crucial;

Each moment and lesson were a necessary part of your *process of becoming.*

You have come too far to turn back now, Dreamer.

You were meant to have a great impact on the collective.

The world needs you in it.

Walk in your purpose, ON PURPOSE!

In pursuit of your promise, Dreamer, be Noah. Your vision, your dream, is your ARK.

Noah didn't know when the flood was coming.

He believed in GOD and built the ark anyway.

He PREPARED!

He trusted in GOD and the process.

He knew that GOD would keep GOD's word.

When Noah took this leap of faith he had to believe in himself as well as his ability to complete the task that GOD had given him.

You see, Dreamer, GOD can give the assignment, but if we do not believe in our ability to carry out the assignment then the process cannot complete itself.

The promise, more often than not, is not realized.

In the pursuit of your promise there will be people who laugh at you.

BUILD ANYWAY!

Some might count you out and leave you in the cold when you need them most.

KEEP BUILDING!

You will encounter setbacks, but trust that things are working in your favor.

Everything that is torn down on the road to your promise, let it go — with love and gratitude.

Everyone who doubted you or didn't support you, they weren't supposed to and it's okay.

You will go on to do great things in spite of the lack of support.

Know that your purpose is rooted in people and bigger than politics.

Stay focused on your promise and keep going.

NEVER QUIT!

Lastly Dreamer, I will leave you with this final thought:

Think about all of the things that you have been through to get to this point; You have overcome so much.

In spite of it all you kept going.

Congratulations, Dreamer!

<u>You have proven that you have the patience that the promise requires.</u>

KEEP GOING!!!

2

FAKING IT IS NOT A REQUIREMENT FOR MAKING IT

DEAREST DREAMER,

Believe it or not, the world existed before the internet became a thing.

There was a time when kids chose playing outside over playing video games.

Not being allowed outside was considered a form of punishment for most kids when I was growing up.

We drank water from the water hose out back and played in dirt.

I know I sound like an elder, reminiscing about a time long gone.

It was a time when people respected one another and things seemed to be simpler, at least compared to now.

It is not my intention to talk about how much things have changed.

I guess it was my *long-winded* way of saying that there was a time before social media and things were a lot simpler.

Now, everything you want is at your fingertips and cutting corners feels like a part of the process.

I existed in a moment in time before there was a silent pressure to convince the world of our happiness or success.

Now we use social media to chase validation from others, like hits of dope; always itching for the next fix, the next *like, comment* and / or *share*.

Authenticity is a rare thing these days, Dreamer.

Social media has created a world full of smoke and mirrors and whether we want to admit it or not; we all play *the game*.

The time will come when your image is the most important thing to you and what something looks like will be more important than what it actually is.

You will become comfortable in your mask.

Somewhere along the journey you will begin to believe that faking it is a requirement for making it.

IT IS NOT!

In some ways you believe that adapting to this mindset is a part of the process of *paying your dues*.

Somewhere you picked up this idea that it was better to fool people into believing you are *this* or *that*, until you actually **become** *this* or *that*, than it was to put your head down and do the work.

You will go into a lot of spaces feeling like an imposter, like a little kid in dress clothes that are too big.

There will be moments when you lose yourself and completely forget who you are and what you stand for.

In those moments, try not to beat yourself up, Dreamer. This too, is a part of the process.

It is a part of *your* process.

You spent so much of your life trying to fit in;

You don't know how to be authentic and it shows.

This will have a significant impact on your ability to build and sustain relationships.

It is exhausting when you have to wear the mask, isn't it?

In the beginning, it is comfortable because it hides the real, authentic version of you and presents a barrier of false protection.

It keeps you in control of just how close others are allowed to get.

You tell yourself that very few people will ever know the real you, as if it is some *point of pride.*

What do you do when the party has ended and the mask you once wore has lost its usefulness.

How will you find your center again?

How will you even begin to sift through the rubble after the tower has fallen and the façade comes tumbling down?

You will finally come to the realization that the sounds you believed were sweet music were actually alarms going off to warn you of your impending doom.

I have good news, Dreamer!

The day will come when you decide that you will operate in your authenticity.

When that day comes, it will be scary, and you will want to turn and run the other way, but you won't.

You will step into your authenticity and take up space in the world in a way that only you can!

Shine your light without apologizing to those who cannot stand its brilliance.

When you are authentic you will find that you attract those who will bask in your radiance and you in theirs; your authenticity finally mirrored back to you by another.

You will connect with souls that make you feel so alive that you want to write a song about it!

You will meet people who see you and appreciate you for who you are.

Most importantly, you will have a greater appreciation for yourself, who you are and what you have been through to get this far.

When you fake it until you make it, everything around you is **FAKE**, *especially the people.*

Especially YOU!

Don't be too quick to judge them for their behavior, after all, they **are a reflection of you**.

They see your greatness but they also see how unaware you are of your greatness.

This will create an opportunity for people to use you, taking advantage and silently tearing you down in an attempt to make you doubt yourself.

They will remind you at every turn that you are wearing your mask and snuff out any attempts you make to try and genuinely express yourself.

The truth, that they don't want you to discover, is that your power lies in your authenticity.

Perhaps it is the very thing that fuels your inner light and allows you to shine with grace and style.

You are fearfully and wonderfully made.

You are a rare and beautiful occurrence.

You are a brilliant and vibrant light in this world.

When you begin to operate as your authentic self, you are an example to others as well, and without even being aware of it, you will commit the highest human act, Dreamer.

You will *INSPIRE* another!

KEEP GOING!!!

3
FAILURE FEELS FINAL...IT IS NOT!

DEAREST DREAMER,

Guess what?

On the journey to your promise you will *fail*.

In short – most times things will **NOT** go according to your plan.

The sooner you accept this and learn to adapt, the better off you will be.

The good news is that failure is a part of the process and although it may feel like it right now, please understand that failure *feels* final, but it's **not**!

Each new day brings with it an opportunity to continue pursuing your promise.

You will encounter moments of failure that knock the wind out of you.

Some of those experiences will send you running the other way with your tail between your legs.

Don't quit.

You may have to retreat and pull back at times, but don't give up.

Your promise is waiting.

Allow the process to complete itself and trust that it will do so.

Trust that everything will work out in the end.

As you sift through the rubble of the tower that is the dream you are building, remember that your failures are the bricks used to lay a strong foundation that will support your future growth and success.

Failure is essential to your process and will result in your promise resting on a foundation that is tested and proven.

The more you fail, the greater your success will be.

The trick is to not give up when things get tough.

Never give up on yourself and your dreams.

Your vision is possible.

Rest assured that any endeavor that goes *down in flames* along the way will light your path as you continue your journey.

Remember that every perceived failure comes with an opportunity to build something better; **something more sustainable**.

It is also an opportunity to gain a new perspective.

Every failure that you survive will be the part in your story where it looked like the end, like all was lost, **BUT GOD!**

The reason that the process requires so much patience is because when you step out on faith, things tend to ebb and flow, A LOT!

You will experience so many ups and downs, and the down times will seem to drag on forever, while the good times feel short-lived.

Learn to prepare and capitalize on those moments in the palace in order to cushion the blow that comes with occupying and navigating the pit.

What is the pit, you ask?

It is a hell, located somewhere between poor fortune and the Valley of the Shadow of Death.

It is a special kind of hell for those who are brave enough to take the leap of faith that is required to realize their promise.

You will find yourself here often during your journey.

It will take you some time, but eventually you will realize that your time in the pit will be your greatest blessing.

The pit will reveal your friends as well as your hidden enemies.

It will show you the people in your life who are really for you and expose those who never were.

The pit will break your heart and correct your vision.

It is necessary.

Even as I am writing this, BluLight Consulting, my firm, is experiencing financial failure. It is a low point and this failure feels very final.

I know in my heart that it is not.

It is only a moment, and this moment too shall pass and another moment will come.

Is there such a thing as a better moment?

Or is the moment only made better once we decide to make the best of the moment we find ourselves in?

Each moment is a blessing, Dreamer.

Do not take them for granted.

Each moment is a stepping stone to your promise.

Each step adds up.

Whatever the setback may be, remember that it is only temporary.

In those moments, where you are unsure and it seems like everything is falling apart, prepare for your comeback.

Get ready; your hard work is about to pay off!

Understand that each failure was then, and is now, a necessary sacrifice.

Failure is the result of trying to do something bigger than yourself.

Remember that you are in pursuit of something greater.

There will be moments when you will feel hopeless but stay focused on why you started this journey in the first place.

You are doing great, Dreamer!

KEEP GOING!!!

4

NOTHING FOR MY JOURNEY

DEAREST DREAMER,

What if I told you that the day would come, when you would look back over your journey, see how far you've come and be glad for every single moment you *lived* through?

When that moment comes, *and it will*, you will finally understand why certain things had to happen the way that they happened.

You will laugh, even at the painful moments, releasing tears of grief and joy for all you've overcome and endured in your pursuit.

Find gratitude for each moment, for every win and every perceived loss.

One day you will find yourself in a space where GOD's promise was kept and every tear you cried was counted.

For each tear, a blessing is attached.

Maybe where you find yourself in this stage of your life makes it hard for you to believe in your promise, Dreamer.

Maybe you feel like you can't win, or life has dealt you a hand that you feel is unfair.

You feel like life has you in a chokehold right now but that's just a feeling, it is not a fact.

Your faith will begin to waiver.

BUT it won't *die*!

Life is but a collection of brief moments and before we know it, we have reached the end of our time here.

When that time comes, Dreamer, be sure the person you meet on your deathbed is not the version of yourself that you *could have been*.

Be sure to take time to enjoy the journey. Take it all in and appreciate it.

Truly experience the people you meet along the way and take them in too.

They will teach you some valuable lessons.

Some of those lessons will be painful.

I heard somewhere recently that you can choose to focus on the people and how they hurt you or you can focus on the lessons they taught you.

Choose to focus on the lessons.

Your power lies in the wisdom you take from the experience.

Don't be in such a rush to reach your destination or a desired point in time, that you miss opportunities to connect with incredible people.

Seize the moments and take advantage of them.

Engage in *genuine, authentic,* unbridled **human** *interaction.*

Create memories.

Keep going and one day you will look up and realize that the life you built made every hardship worth it.

You may or may not cry tears of joy, but there is one thing I am certain of, Dreamer, **you will be grateful for the journey.**

So grateful for each part of the journey that **if someone were to ask you if you would change any of it,**

Your answer would be, *no,* because you understand the importance of every moment and the role that each moment played in your process of becoming.

A collection of lessons and experiences that you have converted into what I like to call *"lived wisdom."*

You will be glad that you kept going.

You will be grateful for all of the characters that you met along the way.

Those characters are a part of your story, playing their role perfectly and guiding you along your path.

Be grateful for all of them.

Rest assured, Dreamer, that one day you will be able to rest and know what it is like to let your guard down a little bit and enjoy the fruits of your labor.

Discover what else your journey has in store for you.

Your tribulations will lead to triumphs if you don't quit.

This journey was specifically designed for you, Dreamer.

You have a mission to carry out on this earth.

You are called to do something great!

Embrace the journey.

Fall in love with the process.

Love the lessons and those who teach them!

KEEP GOING!!!

5
PREPARATION

Dearest Dreamer,

In order for success to be achieved, opportunity and preparation must first be introduced.

Like anything else in life, this introduction is a process.

The process prepares you for your promise.

Trust the process.

Understand and believe that the process will complete itself as long as you do your part.

I'm sure you remember the scripture: *faith without works is dead*.

The purpose of the journey is preparation.

You are being prepared for all the things that come with your promise.

The bigger your vision, the more hardships you will encounter.

Don't let the hardships stop you from taking that leap of faith.

Remember that this journey was created specifically for you.

You will unlock parts of your soul that you didn't know existed.

You will overcome your fears and become more self-reliant.

You will not build your vision alone, but **you will know that you can bet on yourself and GOD,** even if the help of man is nowhere to be found.

Opportunities will come.

Some will be building blocks for you, while others will be distractions.

With each comes the option to choose.

Here is a secret; it doesn't matter which option you pick because each will prepare you in some way for your promise.

Along my path, I learned that perspective is important. Understand that the way that you see things, matters.

What is the story that you tell yourself?

Do you pursue your dreams with this little voice in the back of your head telling you that everything you're working to build is going to fall apart?

Perhaps that same voice is telling you that you will never realize your vision or live in your promise.

THESE ARE ALL LIES!

Your promise is yours as long as you believe in it and continue to do the work.

As someone who has believed in my promise for a long time, I can assure you that if you don't possess the patience that your promise requires, you will find yourself frustrated and tired.

In some cases, the thought of giving up on your vision will seem like a great idea and a welcomed relief.

Understand that the circumstances you find yourself in are only temporary.

Although this experience may not feel like it's temporary, trust me when I tell you that *IT IS*!

Each moment brings with it an opportunity to change or to stay the same.

Choose to evolve.

Grow through what you go through and rise from the ashes like the beautiful phoenix that you are.

You are being prepared for GREATNESS.

Allow the process to unfold and rest assured that everything is working for your good!

You may feel as though you are ahead of your time.

You have great ideas that always seem to fall flat or lose steam.

One day you will have an opportunity that will be the culmination of all the opportunities that you thought didn't work out.

On that day you will understand that every moment prepared you for this moment.

Understand that nothing that you've been through is a waste, Dreamer.

It is not a loss or a lesson, it is an experience; a beautiful stroke of genius across the magnificent canvas that is your life.

Your preparation is not in vain.

The things that are in store for you are beyond your ability to imagine.

Things will work out even better than you thought they would but, only if you keep going.

Move forward through all of the dark nights, frustration, isolation and pitfalls; keep going and the struggle will all be worth it.

GOD counted every tear!

<u>Those same tears will be used to fill your cup until it RUNS OVER!</u>

Be thankful, Dreamer.

Thankful for every moment that led you to this moment of *now*.

The very things that you thought were **breaking you** were actually **making you**.

Find a space in your heart and soul where you hold only gratitude for your experiences.

You are equipped and fully supported.

Go forth and do great things!

You will have an incredible impact on this world.

Understand that you are always walking in your purpose, even when it doesn't look or feel like you are on the right path.

Be grateful for all that comes with being prepared for your promise.

Understand that *promise without preparation will result in a perpetual cycle of disappointment.*

Prepare yourself!

KEEP GOING!!!

6

CALLED TO INSPIRE

Dearest Dreamer,

What I am about to tell you might ruffle a few feathers.

Understand that I am speaking from my own experience, and in *my* experience, obtaining a degree was not required in *my* process of becoming.

I am fortunate to have the life that I have and to do the work that I love to do.

I am grateful.

It didn't come without struggle; lots of struggle, some hard lessons and a little heartbreak.

My point, Dreamer, is that the same thing that was true for me might also be true for you.

Perhaps you have a gift that doesn't require you to pursue a degree or any sort of training.

There is so much pressure to follow certain paths due to guarantees of security and success.

Remember that your path is yours, and it is okay to choose a path that is not aligned with whatever may be considered the *standard* path or course to success.

Want to hear something funny?

There is no standard path to success.

There is only *your* path.

Success is yours to define.

Don't ever give that power to others.

You are destined for greatness.

Your promise will come with many paths, Dreamer.

I am here to tell you that all those paths lead you to the same place.

Don't let anyone tell you that you can't do something.

It took me a while to understand that the people who told me that I couldn't do it, didn't do so out of spite; they were speaking from a place of fear.

Those people were projecting their fears on me.

Those same people would wither under the weight of your promise, giving up on the path long before reaching this point.

I spent a lot of time trying to fit into the box that others built for me.

That box was really a coffin.

I didn't understand that I had already been qualified by the **MOST HIGH**.

GOD created me with intention and the same is true for you.

Before you started this journey, it was destined for you to become the person you are currently evolving into.

Even when it feels like you are off the path, you are not.

There will be those who tell you that you can't do it.

They will say that you don't have enough experience.

You didn't go to school for that...Your family has always done this...or no one in your family has ever done that...

Choose your path.

As a result of your choice, you may have to go through a lot of your journey alone.

That is okay.

Find **solace in the solitude** and **inspiration in the isolation.**

These are the moments that will make you.

In these moments you will discover new parts of yourself and re-discover parts of yourself you thought long dead.

You will need **all** parts of yourself in order to fulfill your destiny and complete your assignment.

You were fearfully and wonderfully made for such a time as this, Dreamer.

Your journey will come with highs and lows and there will be moments along the way where you are so beat down, you can't see the blessings that are right in front of you.

In those moments, find something to be grateful for and then another thing and then another, until your heart is heavy with joy and anticipation for what your future holds.

Your gratitude will attract more.

More importantly, it will help you to reset and remember what is important.

Don't lose sight of your vision and allow your setbacks to shrink your dream.

Go forth boldly with a **pure purpose** and **clear vision; take inspired action.**

Avoid all risks and take only *leaps of faith.*

Remember that GOD is always with the underdog.

When the time comes and you are no longer the underdog, aspire to be the instrument that GOD uses to bless, uplift and empower the underdogs coming behind you and those that you encounter along your journey.

Dream and pursue your dreams without a need or desire for outside validation.

Do things that inspire you, and I promise that you will inspire others.

Lastly, I will leave you with this, Dreamer.

When the time comes and you are living your dream and have accomplished all that you set out to do, **don't let it go to your head**!

Let your work speak.

Let your fulfilled dreams speak.

Let the impact that you have on the lives of others, SPEAK.

KEEP GOING!!!

7
THE ENEMY

Dearest Dreamer,

If you remember nothing else, remember this:

Immediate gratification is the enemy of sustainable, long-term growth and success.

You must know that building something impactful takes time, effort and faith.

Every promise requires patience.

The journey prepares you to withstand the weight of your vision.

There will be opportunities to cut corners and take the easy way out, but you won't.

There is something deep down inside you that knows that the struggle will be worth it in the end and that your suffering is not in vain.

You think that you want everything all at once, but the truth is that you don't.

Don't skip the crucial steps that are a part of your journey, trying to reach a destination that is ever-evolving and non-existent at the same time.

Believe that what you desire, you will have in due time.

Continue to work and make decisions that reflect where you are trying to go.

Avoid making choices that are rooted in where you have been, what you have been through and the circumstances that you have overcome.

There will be times where things just fall into place and work out for you without any setbacks.

I squandered most of those opportunities and there is a good chance that you might do the same thing.

I didn't understand the importance of **showing up** and leveraging the opportunity to secure my next opportunity.

I'm not saying that you should only work hard to secure your next opportunity, but I am telling you that *each opportunity that you show up for is an invitation for another opportunity to present itself!*

I wasted a lot of time regretting past decisions and the opportunities that I didn't appreciate.

I wasn't supposed to appreciate them.

If I didn't squander the opportunity then how would I appreciate or learn to manage the next opportunity that had the potential to change my life?

There will be moments when you feel like you are spinning your wheels and getting nowhere.

Have faith that you are covering ground.

This journey will exhaust you.

It will leave you feeling hopeless.

It will chew you up and spit you out— if you let it.

This journey is not for the weak-hearted or for the timid.

This journey was designed for the bold and brave souls who are willing to be wrong; to fall and continue to get back up and move forward.

I can tell you that after ten years of building, tearing down and rebuilding again, I have learned some invaluable lessons.

I find myself in this space of complete and utter gratitude; gratitude for my journey, and gratitude for the lessons and the people I met along the way.

Even when you don't understand it, Dreamer, believe that all things are working for your good.

There is nothing wrong with taking your time to build your vision.

I know it can be hard sometimes, but don't compare your journey or progress to another's.

It is a waste of your energy.

Believe that your journey was specially designed for you, and everything that is meant for you will manifest in your life.

Build slowly.

Build with faith.

Build with intention.

Don't give up, Dreamer.

KEEP BUILDING!

Today I faced my worst enemy and a harsh truth.

The enemy was me.

<u>*The truth was that I was holding myself back.*</u>

There will be times along your journey where you feel like the world is against you.

It will feel like your enemies, both real and imagined, have conspired against you to keep you out of certain places and spaces.

You will be angry and then sad but you won't be defeated even on days where you may feel defeated.

Rest and reset, Dreamer, and after you have taken a moment to catch your breath;

KEEP GOING!!!

8

ELEVATION, ISOLATION, DOMINATION

Dearest Dreamer,

There are stages in the process of becoming.

You don't just get to skip ahead to what you believe is *the good part*.

The truth is that **the journey, in its entirety, is the good part!**

Be careful what you wish for, elevation is painful at times and requires you to step outside of your comfort zone.

Elevation has its own set of requirements, and one of those requirements is being isolated.

No one wants to be isolated.

We are all taught the importance of companionship with everyone, except ourselves.

Understand that the connection you have with yourself is the most important connection.

The connection that you have with yourself is important because it informs every decision that you face at each of the crossroads you encounter along your path.

You will choose to sever certain connections and move away from people.

It won't be easy but remember that it is okay to outgrow a person, place or thing.

Elevation will require separation.

It will require you to surrender; to let go and move on.

As you shift your thinking from your old perspective and operate in your understanding, learn to be okay with being disliked, misunderstood, judged, ridiculed and overlooked.

Continue on your path and don't lose your faith.

Now is the time for you step outside your comfort zone but don't worry, that's the territory where blessings, growth and expansion dwell.

You're going to be *extremely uncomfortable* and there will be times where you doubt yourself or think that maybe you made a mistake.

The only mistake you will make is believing that these feelings are not normal.

Push through the feelings.

They are just feelings for the moment and like the moment, they will pass.

Remember that there is a process that must complete itself for your promise to be realized.

Don't rush that process or you will miss vital lessons and experiences that are meant to help you grow.

Evolve your thinking to go to the next level.

Find **inspiration** in your *ISOLATION*.

It is one of the best parts of the journey, similar to the caterpillar's experience of transforming in its cocoon.

There will be times where your world is going up in flames and you're left buried in the ashes.

Like the phoenix, you will rise from those same ashes a better, stronger, more dominant version of yourself.

You will be grateful for the flames that destroyed you, your world and everything in it that didn't serve you.

Sometimes isolation feels a lot like loneliness.

One day you will understand that this separation is necessary.

A lot of these letters were written in times of isolation and deep reflection.

Here is what I discovered, Dreamer; isolation became more enjoyable for me, as my love for Self grew stronger.

I understand the power of isolation now, and no longer see it as a punishment but a wonderful blessing instead.

There is an interview with Maya Angelou, where she describes a sacred place that we all have inside and how we should keep that place clean, clear, and pristine.

She said: *"This might be the space where you go to meet GOD."*

She describes it as a space that should be *"inviolate"* or unviolated.

For me, that space was discovered and cultivated during my own periods of isolation.

Obscurity is a blessing, Dreamer.

It may not feel like it, but trust me, isolation will make the difference in the long run.

When you embrace the isolation, then and only then will you be ready to dominate.

Domination is the final stage and once you reach this stage you will certainly know it.

First, let me clarify: when I am referring to domination, I don't mean domination over others.

You could use the power of domination to overcome others if you want but that never really works, and in the end, you do more damage than good.

Dominating others is tied to your ego.

Dominating yourself, your inner demons, your shadow, requires a connection with something greater than just yourself.

For me, domination required a mixture of surrender, acceptance, self-awareness and understanding.

Surrender, acceptance, and self-awareness will support you in those moments when you lack understanding.

They will support you in the journey that leads you to understanding.

Accepting that **everything is what it is**, but that is not *ALL that there is*, has helped me to *surrender* even more.

Self-awareness helped to shift my perspective, and I lost my appetite for playing the victim, accepting that at times, I was the villain.

I was able to go within and reflect on my own actions, habits and behaviors and see how they impacted my life and the situations I found myself in that didn't serve me.

I wasn't the victim and in instances where I thought I was, I accepted that I had victimized myself by tolerating certain people, places and things that were toxic.

I'd allowed certain things to go on too long.

This brings to mind another point; perhaps the most important point.

Without self-love, elevation, isolation and domination will lead to destruction, chaos and confusion.

Vulnerability is the lantern that holds your light. It has the ability to uplift and inspire those around you.

When we engage in the highest human act, it demonstrates our ONE-NESS and reinforces the fact that we are all connected.

If you don't do the work to dominate your inner demons, then you will continue to sabotage the blessings that are waiting for you along your path.

Be patient.

Be kind.

Be courageous.

Whatever stage you find yourself in right now, be grateful for it.

Rejoice in it.

Embrace it; it will transform you.

Lean into the discomfort.

***Elevate** your thinking.*

***Isolate** your fears.*

***Dominate** the voice within that tells you that you are not worthy.*

KEEP GOING!!!

9
SURERENDER

Dearest Dreamer,

If you have a need or desire to control everything, then this is going to be a hard experience for you.

Your surrender is required.

You will have moments along your path that will make it difficult to surrender.

You feel like if you give up control, you will lose your grip on life completely and everything will disintegrate.

This isn't true.

In fact, it couldn't be further from the truth.

When things aren't going the way you planned, it is a blessing.

Remember that before you came up with a plan, there was a process.

That process will complete itself in time.

Remember this the next time you want to give up.

Don't feel bad when you find yourself in a space where the struggle is too much.

In those moments, giving up will seem like the right answer.

IT IS NOT!

There were so many times that I wanted to give up.

There were days when I didn't want to get out of bed and even some days when I didn't.

I was flat broke; looking for purpose, searching for peace and praying that better days would be on the other side of the chaos that was my life in that moment.

I needed things to work out but I had **one** requirement.

I had to be in control of the narrative.

I can only describe it as me attempting to tell the story while writing it.

Let go of the way you *THINK* things should play out; surrender and trust that things will work out as they were intended.

When you surrender, you are expressing your faith.

Surrender.

Trust the process.

KEEP GOING!!!

10

ENOUGH IS ENOUGH

Dearest Dreamer,

You.

Are.

Enough.

11

PROVEN

Dearest Dreamer,

We've all done things in life that we are not proud of and sometimes one of the hardest things to do is forgive ourselves.

If you are not careful, you will continue to live in a cycle that was born from your struggles and the time you spent in survival mode.

Give yourself credit for the changes you've made.

Be grateful for your growth and how far you have come.

Don't be desperate to prove to the people you've hurt in the past, that you have changed; the change will be evident in your actions and not your words.

If you are able to make amends, then you should.

It is also important to remember not to take it personal when life reminds you that forgiveness doesn't require reconnection.

Forgive yourself and don't hold feelings of hurt or resentment towards the people who reject you.

Their rejection is protection.

It may not feel that way in the moment but trust me, it's for the best.

We all have a part to play and they played their part.

Understand that another person's refusal or inability to see your growth is not a reflection of you or how far you've come.

They may still be holding onto feelings from past experiences.

It is not indicative of a lack of growth on your part.

People often hold you in their minds the way that they met you or the last way that you showed up in their lives.

Sometimes, if they meet you in the pit of your process, they will treat you like you still carry the stink of the pit, even after smelling the scent you carry now from the baths that you took in the palace.

They will see you as that same person you were when you were living in survival mode.

I am here to remind you that you did then what you knew how to do and now that you know better, you are doing better. (*Maya Angelou*)

Rest in that truth, no matter what the outside world tells you.

Be grateful for each lesson and understand that you were only aligned with those people for a time and it is that version of you that they are using as their point of reference.

They are connected to a version of you that no longer exists.

Remember that it is their point of reference and not yours.

You are not that person anymore.

You have grown.

Keep growing.

Keep living.

Keep giving.

Let GOD and time do the proving.

KEEP GOING!!!

12

TO THYNE OWN SELF

Dearest Dreamer,

I am convinced that if imitation is the highest form of flattery to man, then originality and authenticity must be the highest form of flattery to GOD.

I didn't understand the power of authenticity and how it has the ability to open doors, hearts and minds.

Your authenticity is what gives you the power to connect with and inspire others.

I used to believe that I was destined to be a loner;

That no one would accept the good, bad and ugly parts of me.

This was probably because I couldn't accept those parts of myself.

I couldn't accept that I was good because of the *bad* that I had done.

I believed I was bad in spite of the *good* I had done.

The ugliest things I've done, were self-inflicted; done at the expense of myself.

Remember to be thankful for it all!

Each experience is full of lessons and when you apply the lessons it strengthens you and helps you become more aligned with who you truly are.

Be true to yourself and when something no longer serves you, release it with love and gratitude for the lessons the experience taught you.

Be true to yourself and don't go against your own intuition.

Be good to yourself.

KEEP GOING!!!

13
WHILE YOU ARE HIDING

Dearest Dreamer,

While you are hiding and shrinking yourself to fit into places and spaces that you outgrew a long time ago, **someone is out there waiting to be inspired by you.**

Inspired by your gifts.

Inspired by your energy.

Inspired by your authenticity and your vulnerability.

Inspired by YOUR story!

I know that this journey hasn't been an easy one but it has always been bigger than you.

Someone else's dream is attached to yours and your story is the story of perseverance that they need to hear in order to keep going.

I remember going to a friend's church once and at the end of her sermon, she called me into her office to have a conversation.

She told me that while I was *"running around in the world playing, GOD was waiting for me."*

She told me that there were souls attached to my destiny that I knew nothing about and may never meet.

She told me that they needed me to walk in my calling.

I was immediately turned off by the statement and looking for the nearest exit.

I thought that she was trying to force my hand and get me to answer the calling that so many others saw for my life — becoming a Pastor.

I realized after going through my own spiritual journey, that what my friend was trying to say was that GOD gifted me and I was meant to use those gifts to be a light in the world and bring light to others' dark spaces and places.

I remember the feeling that I got in the pit of my stomach when she shared her thoughts with me.

It was a heavy feeling and the weight of it let me know that she was right.

Life and the experiences that come with it will make you think that your story doesn't matter.

Everybody is going through something, so what makes your story so special?

I was constantly asking myself this question.

I have a question for you, Dreamer.

Are you hiding?

If the answer is yes, ask yourself why?

As you read these words, you can feel that same feeling in the pit of your stomach.

That's called resonance.

It is a signal.

Lean into that feeling and then into your gifts.

Stop hiding your light.

It is so vibrant and inspiring.

You've played small long enough.

It's your time now.

It's your moment.

You learned the lessons and you overcame the obstacles.

Now is the time to stop hiding.

Now is the time to express yourself and share your gifts with the world.

You are capable, Dreamer.

GOD knows it and so do you.

KEEP GOING!

14

THE SPACE BETWEEN

Dearest Dreamer,

As I've told you in previous letters, **immediate gratification is the enemy of long-term, sustainable success.**

We have all been trained to focus on the result and not the journey.

We do not realize that the journey is the most important part.

The space between where you are now and where you are trying to go is where growth happens.

It is not going to feel good when you're going through it but trust the process.

Sometimes when you are in the Valley of the Shadow of Death, despair and hopelessness feel like they will never release you from their grip.

Over the years, I've learned to appreciate the space between where I am and where I am going.

Those moments become memories and it is important to take in as much of the journey as you can.

The experiences between where you are and where you are going are crucial.

You need those lessons.

I've spent so many years chasing a moment, and as a result, I have missed out on many moments.

Don't make that same mistake, Dreamer.

All of these experiences are what make your story so powerful.

I know that the twists and turns can be overwhelming at times but it is what makes the story so good in the end.

Every time you push through and overcome obstacles, you add to your strength and prepare yourself for the next level.

The key to moving in the "space in-between" is to learn the lessons.

What's more important than learning the lessons?

Applying them to your life.

Every time you feel like you are being held back, understand that **YOU ARE BEING PREPARED!**

Every time you feel discouraged, understand that **YOU NEED REST!**

Every time you feel disappointed because things didn't go according to plan, understand that **YOU ARE BEING RE-DIRECTED!**

One thing remains the same throughout all of these phases, Dreamer.

YOU ARE STILL MOVING!

KEEP GOING!!!

15
T.H.A.W. (TIME HEALS ALL WOUNDS)

Dearest Dreamer,

I've said it before and I think it bears repeating,

THIS JOURNEY IS NOT FOR THE FAINT OF HEART!

You are going to run into people, places and things that turn you cold to the world around you.

Your heart will be broken.

You will feel defeated.

Remember,

TIME

HEALS

ALL

WOUNDS.

I know that you are angry about some of the experiences you've had along your path.

Allow your your heart to THAW!

You are not there anymore, Dreamer.

You are safe now.

What was done is done and it is okay to move on when things don't work out.

You can't change the past but you can change your present moment by shifting your perspective and taking action towards your vision.

I was recently going through some notes from my podcast, *A Loner's Guide to The Galaxy*.

I never released those episodes and I am glad that I decided to keep them in the *vault*.

I realized that time had healed a lot of those old wounds and that I didn't feel the way I once felt.

I also came to the realization that a lot of those wounds were self-inflicted and born from my lack of self-worth and self-love.

Coming to the realization that *I wasn't there anymore*, felt good.

Whatever the circumstances, I made it to the other side.

Understand that when things happen in your life, Dreamer, they are happening **FOR you** and not **TO you**.

Allow the process to complete itself and continue to show up every day.

Your time will come.

Let that old hurt go.

Move forward in peace, with love and gratitude.

Your destiny is calling and it requires you to have a healed heart.

Keep doing the work, Dreamer.

KEEP GOING!

16

USED INSTRUMENTS

Dearest Dreamer,

Don't get angry when you ask GOD to use you and GOD sends people to do it.

You wanted to be used and you will be.

I spent years being angry about my experiences with people who saw my gifts, talents and abilities and used them for their advantage while I was left with little to nothing to show for my contributions.

I always felt like I never got my fair share.

I became bitter over the years and eventually started to shut down.

I was determined not to share my gifts.

I understand now that I was only hurting myself.

My anger and bitterness were holding me back and if you are not careful, the same will be true for you.

I decided that instead of focusing on the circumstances, I would focus instead on the lessons learned and the knowledge and skills that I gained from those experiences.

So, the next time you ask GOD to use you, don't feel discouraged when GOD sends people to do it.

Understand that you are being prepared.

You are being processed.

The road has been a long one and the journey has been tough, but look at all of the things that have manifested from those experiences.

Who knows, maybe one day you will write a book about your experiences and the lessons you learned will inspire others.

Remember that life is full circle and you didn't miss your moment.

You are living in it and creating it every day.

Your time will come and you will be used to accomplish something greater than yourself.

Your moment will come and you will realize that all those times you were being USED you were actually being prepared to be **USEFUL!!!**

KEEP GOING!

17

THE DISCONNECT

DEAREST DREAMER,

I was reflecting recently and came to the realization that I have lived most of my life based on what the "voice in my head" was saying.

At one point, I believed that it was GOD speaking to me.

Then I thought that perhaps it was my Higher Self guiding me along my path.

I felt silly when I came to the realization that a majority of the things *the voice* was saying were simply thoughts, based on feelings (both processed and unprocessed) from past experiences.

As a result, I was prone to trusting other people and their experiences, thoughts, perceptions, feelings and opinions, above my own intuition.

Eventually, I found myself in a space where I felt disconnected from GOD and people.

I came to realize that you can never be disconnected from GOD.

There were definitely times where I felt misunderstood by man and overlooked by GOD.

It looked and felt like everyone else was moving along their respective paths and I was stuck in the same place, going in circles.

I am grateful to know that I was never standing still.

GOD was carrying me.

I'm reminded of a picture that hangs in my Gran's house called *Footprints in the Sand*.

The image has a set of footprints on a sandy beach. The sun is setting (or rising) and along the side of the picture, there is a poem/story.

The poem or story describes a dream that a man had where he was walking along the beach with GOD.

He describes flashes from scenes of his life being displayed across the clouds in the sky.

In the last scene of his life and during some of his darkest moments, the man noticed that only GOD's footprints were visible in the sand.

He realized that GOD was carrying him through those difficult times in his life.

It reminds me of so many times in my life where I look back and wonder how I made it through?

There are many instances in my life where I **KNOW** that GOD was carrying me.

I am grateful for every hardship.

Every setback was really a set up for a comeback.

One day I was sitting in meditation and GOD spoke to me.

I felt a strong sense of peace, calm and joy.

The voice told me that the voice I heard before and thought was my own was the thing that was causing the disconnect.

Listening to this voice resulted in me finding myself in situations where I thought that I was listening to the voice of GOD, only to be disappointed when things went wrong.

GOD showed me that it was not an *inner voice* but a *feeling* that was guiding me.

It was a **STRONG** feeling; a gut feeling.

I remember key moments where I wasn't sure what would happen next but I had a strong feeling that I felt compelled to follow.

Later, I would get more information through experiences and interactions that let me know that I made the right decision.

I was unable to connect that voice and that feeling in order to understand what was happening in real-time.

Life's experiences taught me how to connect the voice to the feeling.

When I didn't listen to that gut feeling, I found myself involved with people, places and things that did not serve me.

I sometimes stayed in those spaces too long.

Here's a download that I just got as I was writing you this letter, Dreamer.

GOD is in the *FEELING*.

Follow the feelings that bring you peace.

Discover the feeling that is JOY and embrace it with gratitude.

You are worthy, Dreamer.

You are a brilliant light in the world and you will reach your goal!

Above all else, trust yourself and your instincts.

Don't second guess your gut feeling.

Pursue the things that bring you joy and peace and remove those things from your life that do not.

KEEP GOING!

18
CRAZY

Dearest Dreamer,

Let them think that you are crazy.

Anyone who did anything that greatly impacted the world was thought to be crazy at some point in time, so take it as a compliment.

You will have an easier time if you focus less on what people think about you and spend more time thinking about what *you* think about *yourself* and the work you are doing.

When you are a dreamer, you have the ability to see the seed, the tree that the seed will eventually become and the fruit that the tree will bear.

Not everyone has this gift and the sooner you come to this realization, the better off you will be.

One lesson that I wish I knew sooner was to stop telling everyone else about my vision and dreams.

I discovered that often times if you tell your dreams to the wrong people, you will expose your dream to what I call *Dimmers*.

These are people who pose as your allies but the truth is that they don't want to see you win.

They want to stick close to you just in case you *do win* but, in the moments, when it counts, they won't help you.

They will try to make you believe that your idea or vision is crazy.

They will ask you things like, "Are you sure you can do that?"

Your only response to this question should be: **NOTHING.**

These people will slow you down and get it your way if you let them.

DO NOT LET THEM GET IN YOUR WAY!

Remove yourself from their company with love and gratitude for the experiences you had with them and continue to move forward along your path.

KEEP GOING!

19
BEWARE THE DIMMERS

DEAREST DREAMER,

We both know that your inner light is mesmerizing and powerful.

It is bright and warm and it draws people in.

This hasn't served you well over the years, and you let some people bask in the rays of your brilliant creativity who didn't truly appreciate the darkness that makes your light shine so bright.

They became intoxicated by your radiance and before you knew it, they were trying to dim your light.

I call them *Dimmers*.

They can see that you're powerful but not aware of your full power or the potential that your light has to inspire others.

They believe that they can leverage your gifts to help supplement their lack of creativity and originality.

Don't fall into this trap.

Believe that you are more than capable and have the ability to see things through; have faith!

The truth is that your light inspires them and sometimes, often times, *envy is just mis-channeled inspiration.*

You will encounter many people who try to dim your light and distract you with shiny things and new opportunities, but this too is a trick.

Those opportunities and shiny things might distract you for a while and even make you comfortable, but they won't fulfill you.

They won't bring you peace and they certainly won't bring you joy.

If you're not careful, you'll find yourself chasing *Dimmers*, enjoying their company and the comfort zones in which they thrive.

Is it your goal to expand your comfort zone or break out of it?

Your blessings and your destiny exist outside of your comfort zone.

Fear will keep you in your comfort zone; **Faith will sustain you outside of it**.

If your promise exists outside of your comfort zone, shouldn't your goal be to live consistently outside your comfort zone?

Living and walking in your light is not an easy thing to do and it comes with its own set of challenges.

It is meant to be this way.

Go through the fire and you will come out like GOLD!

Remove people from your orbit who are not aligned with your vision, purpose, promise or path and do so with love and gratitude.

Beware of the people who want you to do well but not better than them and try not to be one of those people.

Never horde opportunities and don't block the blessings that belong to others.

Watch out for people who try to convince you that your light is too bright.

Stop building with people who don't want to see you do well and achieve your dreams.

Stop hanging around people who really don't want you around but continue to tolerate you just in case they need you to shine on them or light the way through their darkness.

Stay away from people who will remind you that they gave you water when you were thirsty and food when you were hungry.

Stay the course and the day will come when you learn to protect that light within and channel its brilliance in the right direction.

You will learn to use your light to have a greater impact on the wold around you.

Don't let them dim your light, Dreamer.

KEEP GOING!

20

DO IT SCARED

DEAREST DREAMER,

I have spent most of my life being afraid.

This world can be a scary place but there is still beauty to be found in it.

I remember when I launched my first consulting firm (a decade ago) I was scared but I was also comforted by the fact that I was doing what I felt called to do at that time.

Starting my first business was the greatest thing I have done next to being a dad to my daughters.

When I first started in my career, I was unsure of myself but remained hopeful that if I kept moving my feet, I would eventually reach my goal.

It was a wild ride and I did have some success.

With success comes failure; some might even consider failure a pre-requisite for success.

Losing everything put me right back in that fear space.

I was back in survival mode.

I didn't understand at the time that the failure that I was experiencing was a part of the process.

I didn't embrace the moment.

I accepted that it happened (after a while) and I kept moving forward without taking much time to reflect.

When you find yourself in a situation where failure is the outcome, trust that everything will be okay and is going according to plan.

It is just a part of the process.

It is re-aligning you with your purpose and your promise.

Train yourself to go with the flow.

Don't resist when things aren't going your way. You will waste a lot of time and energy if you focus too much on trying to course correct.

Instead, you should take that energy and do what you feel led and inspired to do.

Remember, Dreamer, there is nothing to fear except being afraid and allowing that fear to stop you from taking action.

Do and **be** and **create** whatever your heart desires.

Remind yourself that your fear is excitement coupled with doubt.

Remove the doubt, keep the excitement and watch things unfold.

Watch the seeds that you planted sprout, and cultivate those opportunities by taking action with intention, love, and gratitude.

Write that book.

Record that podcast.

Paint that portrait.

Launch that business.

Build your vision!

Whatever it is that is pulling you and calling you to express yourself, do it.

No matter what happens along the way, Dreamer, **KEEP GOING!**

21

LEGACY BUILDER

Dearest Dreamer,

I used to refer to myself as a *"Generational Curse Breaker."*

The weight of being a curse breaker is heavy.

A curse breaker is often one who sees a different way; a better way.

They believe that an option exists outside of their current reality.

They believe in the possibilities.

I decided to stop calling myself a Curse Breaker.

I was tired of focusing on the problems and decided instead to turn my attention and efforts to the promise.

The solution lies in the promise.

I decided that I wanted to be a *Legacy Builder* instead of a *Curse Breaker.*

The legacy will break the curse.

Don't stop doing the work.

New curses can gestate in the soil of your *Legacy Garden* and if left unattended, those weeds will impact future generations.

Dr. Maya Angelou once said, *"You have no idea what your legacy will be because your legacy is every life you touch."*

It's a powerful reminder that every interaction counts.

What will people say when you are gone?

What impact did you have on the world around you?

Did you inspire someone else?

Did you uplift and encourage others?

Did you comfort them when they were having a hard time or judge them for their hardships?

Did you support others genuinely or for your own gain?

What will your legacy be?

I have good news, Dreamer.

It is never too late to admit that you made a mistake and decide to be better.

In that moment and every moment after, choose better.

Choose to *be* better.

Choose to *do* better.

Choose to *be* kind.

Choose *joy*.

Choose *YOU!*

Touch lives and leave a legacy that will continue to impact future generations.

KEEP GOING!

22

THE TRIALS

Dearest Dreamer,

Life is a wild ride, isn't it?

This experience is full of ups and downs.

There are twists and turns along the way that will make your head spin.

You are in a dark space right now and everything around you feels unstable.

It is only a moment and it will pass.

Until it does, here is something that worked for me and maybe it will work for you too.

Understand that your life tells a story, Dreamer.

You won't understand your story or its impact until later.

It was designed to be this way.

If you knew everything you would be required to go through in order to live in your promise, you would turn and run the other way.

You would never fulfill the calling on your life.

You would continue to live in a constant state of fear, depression, doubt and bitterness.

Your path is an unpredictable one.

Just when you think you have it figured out, everything falls apart.

It was supposed to fall apart.

It was always a part of the plan.

Even as I am writing you this letter, I'm facing an eviction from my apartment.

I couldn't feel better than I do right now because I see what is happening and trust that it is for my good and will ultimately be a blessing.

I'm grateful for this experience and for this moment because it taught me an incredible lesson about surrendering and living in my purpose.

In the past, I would have spent time and energy playing the blame game and riding the emotional roller coaster that starts with frustration, peaks at desperation and ends in anger and bitterness.

I see now why my entrepreneurial journey has been so tumultuous.

It was destined to be that way in order to get me to this point.

Remember, Dreamer, **the trials make the story**.

Gratitude is what gets you to the other side of the situation because it helps to shift your perspective.

The things that go left and the journey to make them right again or align with your purpose is what makes the story, your story, so powerful.

The trials, setbacks, mishaps, and mistakes, and the story of how you overcame them is what will inspire others.

KEEP GOING!

23
DON'T WAIT

DEAREST DREAMER,

It is 4:33 in the morning, and I have been up since 12:40 AM, thanks to a late nap earlier today.

The past two days have been interesting as far as my sleep pattern is concerned.

I have been hyper-focused on organizing these letters to develop this book.

I've been asking myself why it has taken me so long to finish this project?

Over the years, I have read some of these letters to the team and other people that I trust.

The response has been the same across the board but I still didn't believe it and decided to wait.

What was I waiting for?

The answer is simple.

I was waiting for *validation*.

I didn't understand the danger of waiting for validation.

So many people go their entire lives doubting themselves, their dreams, and their vision.

They die waiting for someone to validate their vision.

Don't make the same mistake.

Don't wait for them to believe in you.

Instead, do the work and keep the faith.

Once you realize your power, and execute your mission, they will have no choice but to believe in your vision.

Don't wait for their approval.

Don't wait for their recognition.

Don't wait for their acceptance.

Don't wait for their praise.

Don't wait for their applause.

Don't wait for their support.

You are going to have a great impact on this world.

Remember that your calling doesn't come without its fair share of resistance.

KEEP GOING!

24
THE JOY OF SILENCE

Dearest Dreamer,

If you have not been isolated yet, prepare yourself.

Understand that this is not a punishment but an incredible blessing.

These moments or periods of isolation are going to strengthen you and prepare you for your destiny.

I remember believing once that I had been abandoned during a time of isolation.

At that time in my life, nothing was working and I felt like I was going in circles.

I didn't have clarity about what I wanted to do with my life.

On one hand, I wanted to be an entrepreneur but in my heart of hearts, I knew I was meant to be a writer.

I wanted to write.

I knew that I was meant to share my creative gifts with the world.

I knew that I was supposed to use my gifts to uplift and inspire others.

There will be many times Dreamer, where you wish time would fast-forward to the *good part*.

I'm here to tell you that ***all of your life is the good part***, even in those moment when you feel hopeless and defeated.

Those feelings are normal.

They are a part of your journey.

Over the past decade, I've been in isolation more times than I can count, and each time, I have come out stronger.

The same is true for you, Dreamer.

The silence that isolation brings will haunt you at first. It will feel foreign to you, and you will mistake your isolation period for punishment and your sacred solitude for loneliness.

Isolation is a blessing.

Shift your perspective.

Understand that your isolation will always precede your elevation.

You are about to go to the next level, Dreamer, and that same silence you used to dread will be a sacred sound to your soul as you continue on your journey.

It will be the space where you drown out all the noise around you, and gain absolute clarity.

Those moments of silence will be your one-on-one time with GOD.

Take this time to re-connect and get clear on your purpose and your path.

Remember that even the fastest, most powerful race cars have to come in for a pit stop eventually.

Take your time and rest.

This journey is a *marathon* and not a *sprint*.

It comes in stages, and each stage builds your strength and prepares you for the next stage.

Embrace the silence and the *outside noise* will sound less like a voice of reason to you and more like what it is...*NOISE*!

Don't focus on the noise.

It means nothing.

KEEP GOING!!!

25
A LESSON IN LEAPING

Dearest Dreamer,

Even if you haven't leapt yet, know that it is in you, and you have the power to do it at any time.

Believe in yourself, Dreamer!

You were created to do this.

You are called to do it.

Take the leap!

I have been leaping since before I started my first consulting firm and remember my first big *leap of faith*.

I was twenty years old at the time, and I had just landed a job at a major financial corporation.

I hated the job but it paid the bills, so I did it until I could 't do it anymore.

There was one thing that I didn't hate about it though, and that was the fact that it allowed me to move out of my mom's house and into my own apartment.

The process of finding my own place was daunting and I wasn't having much success at first.

I was on the phone with my aunt one day and she reminded me that there were some apartments that my great-aunt used to live in that might be a good fit for me.

The apartments were located about ten minutes away from my job.

I decided to drive by one day on my way home from work and saw a *"For Rent"* sign on the corner next to the stop sign.

It was a rainy Fall day; chilly, but not too cold.

I pulled up to the small model-apartment that doubled as the rental office and walked in to find an older gentleman sitting behind a desk.

His name was Jerry.

I introduced myself and we conversed for a while before discussing the available unit.

Jerry told me that I was the fourth person to stop by that day.

He asked me how old I was, and I told him my age and that my next birthday was in January.

He told me he was impressed that I dressed up in a shirt and tie at my age.

I told him that I was dressed up because of my job and went on to tell him the name of my employer.

He informed me that there were a number of other tenants who worked for the same company and the fact that I worked there was a point in my favor.

He asked me if I could keep up with the rent, which was five-hundred and seventy-five dollars a month.

I could afford it and told him that I would fax over copies of my pay stubs and bring the deposit the following Friday when I got paid.

We shook on it and when the day came to drop off my deposit and sign the paperwork, I did.

I was scheduled to move in March and I was beyond excited.

I called a friend of mine named Louis (I call him Lou).

Side note: Some of you may know him as **Adrian Lewis**. *If you don't know who he is, do yourself a favor and check out his music wherever you listen to your tunes; his work is dope!!! "Until Then" is my favorite.*

Anyway, I convinced my mom to let my little brother, Ro, skip school that day so he could help us get everything moved into the new apartment.

After everything was moved in, I dropped off the U-HAUL and took Lou and Ro back to my mom's house, where Lou's car was waiting.

From there, I went back to my new apartment alone and waited for my *special guest* to arrive.

I am not sure where this tradition started but whenever someone in our family moves into a new place, Gran always comes to help them settle in.

Back then, she would drive all the way from Lima, Ohio for this special occasion.

If you know me, then you know how close I am with my Gran.

Since this was my first apartment, I was already excited but the fact that Gran was coming to spend the weekend with me and help me settle in, was the cherry on top.

It was a cold Friday in March.

Gran got to my apartment and we went straight to the grocery store to get food.

I spent most of the money that I saved to cover my moving expenses and all the little things that you forget you need when you are moving into your first place or any place for that matter.

The weekend went by fast and when Sunday came and it was time for Gran to leave, I was sad and didn't want her to go.

The apartment felt empty after she left.

I was reflecting the other day on how I wouldn't have that beautiful memory with Gran if I hadn't taken that leap and gotten that first apartment on my own.

It came with a lot of struggles but I also created some dope memories in that space.

It was the same apartment, with the nook under the stairs, where I started my first consulting firm.

In August of that year, I would take the ultimate leap; the leap that led me here.

It was an incredible experience that I wouldn't had if I had decided to listen to my mom when she told me to wait and save more money before I moved out on my own.

What makes the experiences so valuable are all the lessons I learned from the struggles that I went through in that space.

Embrace the journey with gratitude, excitement and curiosity.

Take the leap and no matter what happens between where you start and where you find yourself in the next moment; **KEEP GOING!!!**

26

I TO I (INSPIRED TO INSPIRE)

Dearest Dreamer,

What inspires me?

Creativity.

To feel inspiration and then channel that inspiration to create something authentic and unique is an incredible feeling.

It is a blessing.

Throughout your journey, Dreamer, there will be people who try to convince you to dim your light.

They will attempt to trick you into believing that the most brilliant aspects of you are weaknesses and not your strengths.

They will try to convince you that your darkness is who you are and your light is merely a figment of your imagination.

Do not believe this.

Shine on purpose.

Believe that you were sent here to illuminate the hearts, minds and spirits of the collective.

Step into your light, Dreamer.

The more you continue to inspire others, the more you will feel inspired.

Continue to strive every day to commit the highest human act.

What is the highest human act?

Inspiring another…

How do you inspire some one else?

Tell your story!

How?

KEEP GOING!

27
THE PANTHER'S INSTINCT

Dearest Dreamer,

Do you think that the rest the world can't see you *playing small*?

It must look so strange to them, to see you, a powerful force, bowing in submission and unsure of your power.

I was meditating a month or so ago and I saw a vision of a Black Panther.

The panther was stalking its prey, crouching in the bushes and waiting for the right moment to strike.

I could sense the panther's raw strength and power.

The panther locked in on its prey and closed the gap between the two, securing its next meal with ease.

The panther could feel the fear and anxiety coming from its prey but possessed the ability to differentiate between its own energy and that of its prey.

It didn't allow the energy of its prey to impact, conflict with or block its killer instincts.

The panther wasn't deterred from its path; instead, it rested in its power.

The same is true for you, Dreamer.

You will feel most alive when you flow with your natural instincts and gifts.

When you flow with your natural creativity and authenticity, you inspire others.

There's that part of you that believes that you will win if you play small.

Nothing could be further from the truth.

Your light is powerful.

It is uncontainable.

It is brilliant.

Trust me when I tell you that your purpose is bigger than you.

Your purpose is bigger than what others think of you.

Learn to differentiate between your own instincts and those of others.

Don't let them get into your head and distract you with noise.

Don't allow them to project their darkness on you in an attempt to dim your light.

Remember who you are, Dreamer.

You ARE THE PANTHER!

KEEP GOING!!!

28

EXIST IN GRATITUDE

Dearest Dreamer,

Be grateful.

You have the ability to create.

Be creative.

You have an opportunity to inspire.

Be authentic.

You have chosen a path that will make you wise.

Be prepared to play the fool and to do foolish things.

You will love being the teacher, only after you have embraced being the student.

Embrace being the student.

Once you accept that there is always something new to teach, it becomes easier to accept that there is always something new to learn.

Life takes you through some ups and downs, and there will be times when you find yourself on shaky ground.

Keep your faith.

If you don't have faith, then find gratitude.

One good thing in your life, be it a person, place or thing, is a blessing.

There will be times along your path where you feel like you are holding on by a thread.

You will want to give up and start to look for a way out, in a desperate attempt to avoid the inevitable – failure.

Did you forget that you chose this path?

You have the nerve to complain about how hard it has been for you to pursue your promise?

Did you feel that way when you set out on this journey?

No!

You didn't even take a moment to pause.

You dove in head first and now you're upset because things are not going according to your plan.

What plan?

Listen, Dreamer, you're in *it* now and by *it* I mean, you are in the *arena*.

You chose the path of the Gladiator.

The best thing you can do now is shut out the noise coming from the stands.

Some will boo.

Some will cheer you on.

Don't concern yourself with either, they can't save you.

Your goal is to live.

Your objective is to come out on the other side of whatever the *arena* throws at you.

Right now, you're in panic mode and it feels like the walls are closing in on you.

Take a deep breath.

Now take a moment and find something to be grateful for.

You woke up this morning – start there.

What about your gifts?

You have gifts, don't you?

Are you not grateful for them?

Have you been using them?

When is the last time you expressed gratitude for a little thing; a small victory?

Slow down and take in the moment.

As you continue along your path remember this, Dreamer, **always be grateful** and **KEEP GOING!!!**

29
I THOUGHT

Dearest Dreamer,

I thought I wanted money.

I wanted PEACE.

I thought I wanted success.

I wanted JOY.

I thought I wanted wealth.

I wanted ABUNDANCE.

I thought I wanted to be understood.

I wanted to EXPRESS MYSELF!

KEEP GOING!!!

30
THE LONELINESS OF DREAMING

DEAREST DREAMER,

You are not a loner.

You are a dreamer and sometimes dreaming can be lonely.

Keep dreaming.

Keep living

Keep working.

Keep believing.

Keep growing.

KEEP GOING!!!

31
THE POWER A MISTAKE HOLDS

Dearest Dreamer,

By now, I'm sure that you have made your fair share of mistakes.

I have certainly made more than my fair share and tried to learn from all of them, although I have to admit that I haven't always been successful in applying the lesson.

Some lessons took longer to learn than others.

I understand that there's power in the mistakes I've made.

The power that mistakes hold is found in the lessons that are *learned* and **applied**.

Don't be ashamed of the mistakes you have made.

They helped mold you into this current version of yourself.

You can't go back and change the mistakes you made.

The best thing that you can do for yourself is accept them and move on.

One day you will see the value in them.

You will appreciate the part that your mistakes played in your process of becoming.

Your mistakes hold power but they should never hold power over you.

They shouldn't stop you from achieving your goals.

It is a part of your story and that story, if told, could help the next person to avoid making some of the same mistakes that you made.

This is why you shouldn't feel bad about the mistakes you've made.

Give yourself grace.

Where you are unable to give yourself grace, allow GOD's grace to be sufficient and made perfect in your weakness.

Your mistakes will not define you but they will be a part of your story; a part of your legacy.

It was always supposed to be this way.

I discovered something recently that liberated me.

Being open about the mistakes I have made, has freed others from the weight of their own mistakes.

Somehow, we get tricked into thinking that we are the only one going through trials and tribulations.

There is nothing new under the sun.

Your story will resonate with someone.

It will help others.

It will save someone's life.

Authenticity is the key.

Stop beating yourself up about what you've done.

It was necessary.

KEEP GOING!

32
WHAT IF?

Dearest Dreamer,

What if I told you that you are on the brink of the greatest success you have ever experienced?

What if everything goes according to your plan?

What if things work out in your favor?

What if that person who is offering to help you, is doing it out of the kindness of their heart and not because they have ulterior motives?

What if that spark of inspiration you just experienced is the thing that leads you to your breakthrough?

On this journey, the question is always *"what if?"*

The options that are presented to you and how you see them is totally up to you; choose wisely.

There will be moments in your life where you are not sure what to do next; trust the process.

When you don't know where to go next, go within.

Remember that most of the world is made up of smoke and mirrors.

The truth lies within you.

Whatever it is that you're trying to get out of life, GOD has already put it in you.

The purpose of the journey is to discover and express the full magnitude of your light.

I know that it feels like life has beat you down and kicked you around.

Remember that you were made for this and are called to fulfill your purpose, Dreamer.

Go within.

Understand that the journey to your promise is your process of becoming, and that process isn't an easy one.

The transition from caterpillar to butterfly is a nasty, sometimes difficult transformation.

I have learned that those messy moments are the moments that you will be most grateful for later when you are sitting across from someone who doesn't have your best interests at heart and it is time to apply the lessons you learned from past experiences.

You will be thankful that you danced with the Devil, because now you recognize his two-step, and you know that he is always a beat behind the rhythm of life.

Pay attention to the rhythm.

Feel the vibration; embrace the frequency and what it is showing you.

The world is changing around you, Dreamer.

What if you are meant to be a part of that change?

What if you are meant to lead the charge?

You are both the starting point and the catalyst for the change you seek to experience in the world.

What if your gift is meant to impact humanity?

What if your light was meant to shine in other's darkness and act as a guiding light as they make their way through the Valley of the Shadow of Death?

You've walked the same path, Dreamer, through the same valley and the same darkness.

What if by shining your light, you inspire another to shine their own and as a result, they inspire another to shine theirs, and the cycle of inspiration continues?

How much brighter would the world be if we all decided to shine a little more?

The next time you discount your potential to have impact, remember that you only need to *impact* **ONE.**

You only need to *inspire* **ONE.**

You've spent so much time overthinking how things could go wrong that you never stopped to consider what might happen if things go according to the divine plan for your life?

What if the Divine plan is the same for all of us?

What if the call on all of our lives is to inspire others?

What if the plan is to impact as many people as you can with your light?

What if you are the hero, you've been waiting for?

What if you don't give up when things get tough?

What if you keep going?

There is only one way to find out, Dreamer.

KEEP GOING!!!!!

33

THE MOUNTAIN MOVES YOU... YOUR FAITH MOVES THE MOUNTAINS

Dearest Dreamer,

The path to your promise is going to be filled with circumstances that are beyond your control, level of comprehension and sometimes, your ability to believe in a positive outcome.

I tell people that if they want to get close to GOD, they should start a business.

There will be moments where you feel low and alone on your journey.

You will see the vision clearly but no one else will.

Remember that the dream was given to you, Dreamer. Others can't see it because they are not dreamers and more importantly, the dream was not given to them.

You will encounter many mountains along your path and in those moments of your life where you are coming down from the peak of the mountain into the valley, be grateful for the challenges that come with the journey.

Know that the challenges you encounter in the valley are strengthening you and preparing you for your next mountain and the climb that comes with it.

Prepare yourself for these moments.

They will push you to your limit.

Remember that the bigger the mountain, the deeper and darker the valley.

The purpose of the mountain is to teach you through experience, that GOD's grace is sufficient and made perfect in weakness.

You were not made to be perfect.

You were made to **be** and **to have impact through being, inspire others through being,** and **embrace others on their journey as they are** *(being)*.

Your faith, if only the size of a mustard seed, has the power to move mountains.

Your faith will sustain you and **you will find strength in consistency.**

Each day you are taking steps towards your promise.

On the days that it feels like you're not making any real progress, trust the process.

Trust that things happen in their appointed time and not before.

Imagine if you would have received what you prayed for when you prayed for it; you would have missed out on so many beautiful experiences and lessons.

If you need proof of this, look to the blessings you have squandered in the past.

Something happens along the journey and I believe it is the most beautiful part of the process.

Along the journey, a shift takes place in the heart and mind.

You realize that your faith really does have the power to move the mountain.

Like the old song says,

"Lord, don't move my mountain, give me the strength to climb... "

The strength you need comes through the act of climbing.

If your faith is wavering, the faith you need will come from **you** being moved by your experiences and the mountain being moved through you but either way, believe that the mountain will not overcome you.

Whether you move the mountain or climb the mountain, you will show generations to come what is possible and both will glorify GOD and prove that GOD's grace is sufficient and made perfect in weakness.

Remember that it is bigger than you and **KEEP GOING!!!**

34
DESTINED FOR DISCOMFORT

Dearest Dreamer,

Let me guess...

You have gifts.

You have skills.

You have talents and abilities.

You are experiencing challenges.

For most of your journey you have been uncomfortable.

It feels like you are going from one lesson to the next lesson; from one trial to another.

You are tired.

Your promise seems like a cruel lie and achieving your goals seems impossible.

Believe that your vision is possible, and it will come to pass.

First you must **embrace the discomfort**.

Growth is being in a constant state of discomfort.

Understand that discomfort, no matter the level of severity, is an indication that you are no longer dwelling in your comfort zone.

You are uncomfortable because you are in a space that requires you to grow into it.

Until you grow into your position, allow GOD's grace to carry you.

Be vigilant and guard your heart.

Remember that you asked for this path long before you got here.

It was specifically designed to draw out the gifts that GOD gave you to share with the world.

Your story needs to be told.

What is a story without a little discomfort?

Even as I am writing this letter, I am in an uncomfortable position.

I am also in the process of transitioning into a better position.

I have discovered the peace that comes with flowing with my life instead of trying to create and control the flow of my life.

The same is true for you, Dreamer.

There is something in you that you know you are called to do.

You know that you're meant to impact the collective and uplift humanity by raising the vibration, shining your light, and sharing your gifts.

You are a beacon of hope to the hopeless.

Step into the discomfort.

Embrace the discomfort.

Anticipate the discomfort.

Recognize that the purpose of the discomfort is to signal your level of alignment or misalignment with your promise.

Remember that your efforts are being supported by something greater than yourself.

KEEP GOING!!!

35
CHOICE IS HOPE

Dearest Dreamer,

When I was a little boy growing up, Gran used to say that *"life was all about choices."*

In Gran's world, there was never an excuse to do the wrong thing when the choice to do the right thing was always available.

Gran would share her life story with us and tell us the things that she went through or saw others go through, the choices they made in an attempt to cope with their experiences or the choices that Gran made to avoid having similar experiences.

She chose something different for herself and as a result, there were experiences that she had as a child that her children never had to experience because of Gran's choices.

She also shared with us the consequences of her choices and the lessons that she learned from them.

For every action there is certainly an equal and opposite reaction.

I was reflecting recently about the journey of building BluLight Consulting.

The journey has been filled with its share of ups and downs, and I have found myself in a depressed state, feeling hopeless at times.

What was I doing?

Was I doing the right things?

We wanted to build BluLight and saw everything that it could be but despite our best efforts, we couldn't seem to get any traction.

I was frustrated, and frustration can be dangerous when action isn't taken.

Your frustration and lack of action has the potential to fester and evolve into bitterness.

I beat myself up about the choices that I made along the way that hurt others and myself.

I didn't understand the blessing in things not going according to *my* plan.

In each of those moments I had a choice.

I could *choose* to see the blessing in a *bad* situation or I could just focus on the *bad* situation.

I have good news, Dreamer.

Even in your darkest and lowest moments, you still have the power of choice.

You always have the power to choose.

There is always hope.

The ability to choose is hope.

The choice to be grateful is hope.

Your gifts, skills, talents and abilities, are hope.

Your dream is hope.

Your vision is hope.

Your passion is hope.

Your empathy is hope.

Your perseverance is hope.

Your **gratitude** is hope.

As long as you have at least one of the things listed above, you have **HOPE.**

KEEP GOING!!!

36

THE ENEMY WITHIN

Dearest Dreamer,

You know what's really holding you back?

The enemy within.

Each of us has an enemy within.

If the enemy without is immediate gratification, then what is the enemy within?

The enemy within is made up of all the things you don't heal.

The boundaries you don't set and the *disrespect from others that you don't address.*

The behavior from yourself and others that hurts you but goes uncorrected.

Your insecurities and perceived weaknesses.

Your un-checked ego.

These are the things that feed the enemy within.

Do the work that is required for you to heal and you will have the power to heal others.

It will be hard work.

It will be painful work.

It won't be painful forever.

Don't feed the enemy within.

Don't stop believing, you're almost there.

KEEP GOING!!!

37
A HOLY WIND

Dearest Dreamer,

I know that you are stressed right now.

I know what it's like to have that pressure on your shoulders all the time, and absolutely no idea what your next move should be.

I know what it feels like to try anything and everything, and experience the feeling of despair when nothing works.

It is a hopeless feeling.

It is a lonely feeling.

It feels like everyone around you can see you drowning but none of them offer to help you.

No one throws you a life saver.

Don't let this make you bitter, Dreamer.

They were not assigned to help you move forward.

I am reminded of a time in my life where everything seemed to be going wrong and my ship was sinking fast.

I know now that GOD's breath was the wind in my sails; **a holy tailwind that propelled me forward when I didn't have the strength to keep going**.

This journey has always been between you and GOD.

Perspective is the machete you use to cut through the jungle of stagnation and hopelessness, and navigate the valleys in your life.

Understand that desperation kills creativity.

Stress kills creativity.

Uncertainty kills creativity.

Shift your perspective.

Frustration fuels creativity.

Lack fuels creativity.

Stagnation fuels creativity.

Shift your perspective.

You are capable.

It is not too late for you!

You are not out time.

If you have fallen, it's time to get back up!

Take your life back.

Your promise is waiting.

Life knocked the wind out of you but GOD is breathing new life into you.

Be grateful for the holy wind in your sails and allow it to propel you forward to your destiny.

KEEP GOING!!!

38
BE

You have an incredible vision.

You see a future for the world that is better than the collective reality we are currently experiencing.

A brighter future is on the horizon.

All it takes is for a few *Dreamers* to stand in their power, shine their light, and share their gifts to raise the vibration.

You were meant to impact the world, Dreamer.

As cliché as it sounds, you really do have to be the change that you want to see in the world.

The world needs your light.

You were called to shine, you beautiful, brilliant soul.

Be kind.

Be authentic.

Be honest.

Be genuine.

Be compassionate.

Be vulnerable.

Be courageous.

EXIST.

TAKE UP SPACE.

BE.

KEEP GOING!!!

39

WHISPERED ACCOMPLISHMENTS AND SHOUTED FAILURES

DEAREST DREAMER,

Do you know who you are?

You are great!

You are capable.

Your discipline is an accomplishment.

Your perseverance is an accomplishment.

You didn't give up when things got difficult.

Your continued courage in the face of adversity and hardship is an accomplishment.

These are all accomplishments that whisper.

Every day, you put in the work to realize your promise, knowing that there won't be an immediate return on your investment.

This is also an accomplishment that whispers.

If you haven't encountered setbacks yet, you certainly will.

Failure is an inevitable part of the journey.

Failure is not your final destination, Dreamer.

Don't you understand that your failures are the parts of your story that will *inspire* others who are experiencing some of the same hardships that you already overcame?

Your failure is a sign that there is something better on its way to you.

What was weak was torn down to be replaced by something stronger.

Don't run away from failure.

Failure has a lot to teach you.

As I write this, I am reminded of the movie *Home Alone*.

Throughout the movie, the main character, Kevin, is running from this old man who salts the sidewalks in the neighborhood.

He walks around with his shovel and his trashcan full of salt, shuffling around in these big snow boots.

I think it's safe to say that the old man would scare most kids; he definitely scared me growing up.

Kevin avoided the old man and ran from him each time he encountered him throughout the story.

In the end, the old man is the one who saves Kevin from the two burglars trying to break into Kevin's house.

Are you running from failure the same way that Kevin ran from the old man?

I know I have.

We try to avoid it.

We never want others to see our failures or shortcomings, so we wear masks and hide behind façades.

Remember, Dreamer, failure isn't something that can be avoided. It is a part of the process.

When you balance your hubris and your humility, you will experience and understand the full magnitude of your power.

You will be humbled and inspired by the magnitude of GOD's mercy and in awe of GOD's power being expressed through your gifts.

Learn to whisper your accomplishments because they will speak for themselves.

Learn to shout your failures because they will inspire others.

Embrace your failures, as they strengthen your foundation and provide opportunities for you to grow.

Don't waste your time and energy trying to convince others to cheer for you and never miss an opportunity to cheer for yourself.

Stay focused.

Be encouraged.

KEEP GOING!!!

40

REMEMBER TO FORGET

Dearest Dreamer,

At some point in your life, you will do things that you are not proud of and this will cause you to look back at your past with a heavy heart or with some degree of shame.

You will go through a period where you believe that the world will never move past your shortcomings or failures.

I was having a conversation recently with a business associate named Ellen, who was telling me about *working memory*.

As she was explaining working memory to me, she used her hand to demonstrate.

She held a pen in her hand and asked me if I thought that she could pick up her computer mouse with the same hand that she was using to grip the pen?

My answer was *no*.

My answer was correct and she could not hold the pen and pick up her mouse at the same time.

Ellen went on to tell me that is was the reason she didn't mind sharing information and ideas on LinkedIn or anywhere else because it freed up space for more ideas and information to flow into her mind.

This resonated with me.

There are so many messages to unpack, but we can save that for another time.

In that moment, what struck me was the fact that I was frustrated with my journey and where things were with my business.

I felt stalled on my path and I wasn't happy about it.

I meditated on why I was having such a hard time and came to the conclusion that I was still holding on to who I used to be.

I was still trying to build a business in an effort to reverse the failure of my first business.

I had a desperate need for a "do-over" and was running into a wall.

I also had a book in me and I wasn't doing the work to get it done. It made it hard to focus on anything else.

I was scattered.

I needed to make room for something new.

I had learned the lessons from my past and I had done the work.

I am still doing the work; that never stops.

I had to realize that I had done enough work to move forward.

Remember.

In order to remember who I am, I must forget who I thought I had to be.

In order to become who I am *destined* to be, I must let go of the idea of who I thought I *would* be.

I am more than I thought I had to be and more than I thought I could be.

Without GOD, I am NOTHING.

Hold on to the lessons and let go of the circumstances that taught you the lessons.

At myYou are not there anymore.

Remember that failure is a part of the process.

KEEP GOING!!!

41
UNDERDOG

DOG

———

GOD

Dearest Dreamer,
You are the underdog.

You have been the underdog.

You will probably be the underdog again at some point.

There is a part of you that will always see yourself as the underdog.

No matter how far you go in life, never lose that feeling.

It is the part of you that will keep you grounded and connected to the people.

Remember that GOD is with the underdog.

Learn to let people count you out.

Remember why you are doing this.

It is bigger than you; it is bigger than the people who counted you out.

Being the underdog is a gift.

It is your advantage.

Every time others overlook you, it is because you are cloaked in the divine protection that comes with being the underdog.

Let them believe you are not formidable.

Allow them to believe that you are incapable.

You have nothing to prove.

Those same people will regret underestimating you.

They will wish that they would have supported you before.

So, harbor no ill will in your heart for the people who played their role and completed their assignment in your life.

The position that they hold in your journey and story is sacred.

They were a part of your breaking process, and even though the experience broke your heart, <u>it didn't break you.</u>

It strengthened you.

Embrace the power of being the underdog.

Move in **silence.**

Move with **purpose**.

Maintain a clear **vision**.

Continue to take inspired **action**.

KEEP GOING!!!

42

THE STORY

Dearest Dreamer,

Your life is a story.

Don't waste your time and energy trying to tell the story as it is being written; the story writes itself as long as you keep living.

If you want to be frustrated, make a plan, stick to it no matter what, and frustration will find you.

There is nothing wrong with having a plan but you have to remain flexible since plans have a way of going bad.

Be grateful for all of life's twists and turns.

What you love most about your favorite television shows are all of the unexpected twists and plot points.

You will experience setbacks and some of them will break you and make you second-guess whether you have what it takes to continue on your journey.

Don't make the mistake of focusing so much on writing the story that you forget to enjoy the experience that comes with living your life and taking it as it comes.

When I took my first big leap of faith at the age of twenty-two, I didn't have a plan. I was just living my life and seeing what would come next.

I knew that something great would come but I didn't know about all of the pitfalls and the setbacks that came with the journey.

GOD's plan for my life and my plan for my life were not always aligned and there were many times where I felt out of sync with the rhythm of life.

I'm grateful that my path was *destined*, and my promise was **guaranteed by my faith and that faith is at work every day**.

The same is true for you, Dreamer.

You were fearfully and wonderfully made for such a time as this.

The story you think you have to write, requires less effort from you than you think.

All you have to do is keep living and doing the work.

Continue to heal and evolve.

Don't stop pursuing your promise.

Your story will be a legendary tale of perseverance, faith, and creativity one day.

Your story will inspire many others.

Your legacy will be measured by the lives you touched with your gifts.

No other soul has the ability to do what you do in the way that you do it.

A unique expression; that is exactly what you are.

Don't let life break you.

Don't let the journey break you.

Don't let the mistreatment you experience at the hands of others break you.

Don't let the naysayers and haters stop you.

Your story is being written, even now, as you read these words.

Remember that it was written.

Your vision will come to pass.

KEEP GOING!!!

43
BEAUTY IN BEING

Dearest Dreamer,

Isn't life a beautiful experience?

I know life comes with its share of trials and tribulations, but isn't it a beautiful experience?

There have been many times that I have wanted to give up.

I didn't feel worthy.

There were times where I didn't think that I was smart enough.

I have experienced the joy that comes with **simply being**.

Being without expectation.

Being grateful.

Being kind.

Being, simply being, as you are, takes courage.

You will spend a lot of time trying to validate yourself using the outside world to measure your success.

This is a part of the process.

How would you know and understand how powerful you are if you never experienced moments of weakness?

You are called by GOD to impact the world and **be a light** in it.

Your light is meant to shine in other's dark spaces but you must learn to shine in your own dark spaces first.

Back in 2016, I had an experience that inspired this letter.

When I have the time I like to make music playlists.

I create mixes that I think are dope and they usually reflect where I am in the moment or at that point in my life.

Every Friday, I get up and check out the new album releases on Apple Music.

I look forward to zoning out on my work while listening to something that someone else was inspired to create.

I was scrolling through the new releases one Friday, and I didn't see anything that I liked.

I thought to myself how all the new music released that day was "*trash.*"

I immediately corrected myself in the moment.

What made me assume that the music was trash?

How could I so easily dismiss the work of another creative?

Were they not brilliant souls who were inspired to create a body of work, and then brave enough to share that work with the world?

Who was I to judge them?

Who was I to dismiss them and disregard their work?

Writing these letters and publishing them has given me an appreciation for the process of sharing the work.

Once the work is out there, you have to let it **be**.

It can be an intimidating experience.

I continued to scroll through the albums until my eyes landed on a project by Shae Universe called *Love's Letter*.

It is an incredible body of work!

I was inspired by it, and I immediately developed an appreciation for how it was all put together.

I listened to it for an entire day on repeat.

It was a beautiful experience and reminded me that the process of creating something and then sharing it with the world is the most courageous thing a person can do.

It is admirable.

When my family and I visit Destin, Florida, we like to collect seashells whenever we go to the beach.

The last time we were there, I took a moment to appreciate the beauty of each individual shell.

I tossed the shells that I didn't want back into the ocean without ever thinking of any of them as trash.

Dreamer, as you continue along life's beach, be sure to take time to appreciate the beauty of the light and the dark.

Don't force yourself to be one thing or another.

Instead, find gratitude in simply being.

Embrace being.

You are here for a reason.

Continue to shine your light and inspire others.

KEEP GOING!!!

44
COLD WATER

Dearest Dreamer,

Be grateful for every moment that breaks your heart and corrects your vision.

Be grateful for every moment where life splashed cold water in your face and shocked you back to reality.

I call these *"cold-water moments."*

The experience can be unpleasant but the results are worth it.

Cold-water moments give you absolute clarity, and awareness of yourself and the people, places, and things around you.

If you are open to the process, cold-water moments can create powerful shifts for you.

I've experienced many of these moments in my life and I am grateful for all of them.

Sometimes the cold water hits you in the moment, and sometimes it takes years before the moment of realization happens, but know that the moment will come, and when it does, embrace it!

Don't let your ego trick you into missing the lesson that the moment is trying to teach you.

Be open to correction.

These moments are the best kind of correction.

Be grateful for the lesson.

KEEP GOING!!!

45
P.O.W.E.R.

P – PERSECUTED | POWERFUL

O – Ostracized | Original

W – Wounded | Warrior

E – Envied | Elevated

R – Rejected | Restored

Dearest Dreamer,
Your power is measured by your ability to perse-vere through each of the experiences that I outline below.

You will be *persecuted*.

KEEP GOING!!!

You will be *ostracized.*

KEEP GOING!!!

You will be *wounded.*

Heal; and after you heal,

KEEP GOING!!!

You will be *envied.*

KEEP GOING!!!

You will be *rejected.*

KEEP GOING!!!

You are **powerful!**

You are **original!**

You are a **warrior!**

You are being **elevated!**

You are being **restored!**

KEEP GOING!!!

46

THE COMPANY THAT MISERY
LOVES TO KEEP

Dearest Dreamer,

Who told you that you weren't allowed to make mistakes?

Where did you get the idea that you had to be perfect?

The goal was never to be perfect, it was to find peace; it was to discover the joy that is found in simply *being*.

This is freedom.

<u>FREE PEOPLE ARE NOT MISERABLE PEOPLE.</u>

The ultimate goal is to avoid being the company that misery loves to keep.

There will always be something to complain about, and if you are not careful, you can easily get caught in the trap that comes with misery's invitation.

Don't accept the invitation to keep misery company.

No matter what you are going through right now, remember that joy is on the other side of your current circumstances.

The good news is that you are the key to your liberation.

Even as you read these words, life is in the process of pulling out of you what GOD put in you.

Find peace in solitude and mind the company you keep.

Remember that bad company corrupts good character.

Protect your promise.

Protect your energy.

Protect your peace.

Don't be the company that misery loves to keep.

KEEP GOING!!!

47
MY WORST ENEMY

Dearest Dreamer,

Today I came to the realization that I am my own worst enemy.

The same is true for you: you are your own worst enemy.

No one can beat you up about your mistakes and shortcomings better than you can beat yourself up about them.

Don't you see how incredible you are?

Don't you believe in your promise anymore?

It doesn't matter if others doubt you.

It only matters if you doubt yourself.

It only matters if count yourself out.

It has always been **YOU** versus **YOU**.

Overcome the enemy within and continue to do the work.

The enemy within feeds on your fear.

Overcome the fear to overcome the enemy.

You are capable, Dreamer.

Continue to walk in your purpose until you are living in your promise.

KEEP GOING!!!

48
RIGHT PERSON, WRONG ROOM

Dearest Dreamer,

I used to feel uncomfortable in my own skin.

Most of the time, I felt like an imposter and in most cases, I was.

I was constantly trying to show up how I thought others saw me instead of just showing up and being myself.

I was always trying to adapt to the room instead of focusing on being myself in the room and allowing the room to adapt to me.

I spent some time in the wrong rooms with the right people and even more time in the wrong rooms with the wrong people.

I understand now that none of those people were actually the *wrong* people.

The rooms and the people were all RIGHT.

They helped to prepare me and I am grateful for the experiences.

It was a requirement for me to go through certain experiences with people in order to elevate.

Be who you are and you will continue to attract *like*-energy.

What is meant for you will find its way into your orbit.

You will attract some darkness; be sure to use your discernment.

Be open to experiences and try not to take anything personal; it's never personal.

If you are operating in your authenticity then you are the right person, in the right place, at the right time, with the right people, in the right room.

Embrace the experiences as they are uniquely designed to prepare you for your promise.

Your journey is inspiring someone else and you don't even know it.

KEEP GOING!!!

49
GRATEFUL SURRENDER

Dearest Dreamer,

When you reach a low point in your journey, it can be hard to keep going.

You may be in a space where you want to give up.

Your only desire is to find balance and peace in your life.

The stress is mounting and it feels like it's too much.

I understand.

Sometimes this journey and the experiences that come with it feel like doing a trust fall with GOD.

Every time I thought GOD dropped me or let me fall, I quickly realized that the resistance I was experiencing was a result of me trying to control the outcome instead of surrendering to the Divine plan.

Learning to surrender and go with the flow, changed my life.

In *survival mode* it can be hard to surrender.

Surrender requires a feeling a safety before you can release control.

The control you think you have, Dreamer, is an illusion.

You are on your path and you will encounter some falls along the way.

You will fall and hit rock bottom a few times.

Even in those moments, **_especially_** in those moments, GOD will catch you.

When you don't know what else to do and things are out your control, go within to discover the answer.

Some call this prayer and some call it meditation.

Perhaps the two things are the same thing.

When you go within, you are safe.

You are safe to surrender.

Surrender is peace.

Surrender is joy.

Surrender is clarity.

Surrender doesn't mean that you are giving up the pursuit of your promise, it means that you have given up the idea you had of how things would play out.

Release yourself from the bondage of your expectations and surrender.

Allow life to unfold.

KEEP GOING!!!

50
THE MIRROR EXPERIENCE

Dearest Dreamer,

You have been through some things that you couldn't control, and because of this, you got very good at mirroring others in order to survive.

There was a time when the most important thing to you was fitting in and being accepted by others.

Do you remember how uncomfortable it was to wear the mask all the time?

You learned to laugh when nothing was funny and to scratch when you had no itch.

You got good at playing the *mirror game.*

What happens when you are alone in a room one day and catch a glimpse of your own reflection?

Will you recognize yourself?

Will you be proud of the person looking back at you?

If you are not, **will you change?**

An opportunity has presented itself, Dreamer.

It is time for you to go to the next level.

It is time for you to elevate your thinking.

Don't harbor any ill feelings towards the people from your past who mistreated you.

Most of them were on assignment.

Their assignment was to be your mirror.

You attracted them into your orbit because you were just like them and they looked just like you.

You were comfortable with them while you were in your comfort zone.

Now that you are living outside of your comfort zone, you can clearly see the misalignment.

You try to hold on and keep the connection alive but despite your best efforts, the connection dissolves.

It was supposed to; this is all a part of the plan.

One day you look up and realize that you no longer see your reflection in the people, places and things around you.

Simply put, they don't resonate anymore with this ever-evolving version of yourself.

It is okay to move on when you no longer see your reflection in the mirror, Dreamer.

Perhaps the absence of you reflection is a sign that you have moved on already....

Release those people, places and things with love and gratitude.

Do not judge them.

To judge them is to judge yourself, Dreamer.

They are a part of your story now and no longer a part of your life; it was for the best.

You will meet new people along the way and they too will teach you invaluable lessons.

Don't be afraid to look in the mirror.

Don't miss the opportunity to realize that *your* world is a reflection of *you*.

KEEP GOING!!!

51
PLAY IT FAIR

Dearest Dreamer,

I haven't always played it fair and I haven't always done the right thing.

I haven't always operated in truth, love and integrity.

I was raised to know right from wrong, and sometimes I chose wrong because it was convenient and seemed easier than continuing to struggle.

There was some part of me that believed that it didn't matter how I got to my end result as long as I was *"winning"* in the moment.

I wanted to **win**.

Life has shown me that there is no shortcut to your promise.

There is no fast way to manifest your vision.

The only option is to do the work and keep the faith until your promise has been fulfilled.

In my haste to find success, I was willing to fast-talk anyone willing to listen and no bridge was too big to be burned if I believed it was in the way of my success.

I didn't understand the power of relationships.

I didn't play it fair.

There was a part of me that believed that I couldn't afford to play it fair, after all, life hadn't played it fair with me; at least that's what I told myself.

You are in a situation right now, Dreamer, where you have the choice to *play it fair* or take the shortcut.

Play it fair.

Don't take the shortcut.

You prayed for patience.

The delay is a teaching you to be patient.

Be patient.

Your time will come, Dreamer.

Continue to grow.

Keep healing.

Keep building.

Keep doing the work and having faith in your promise.

Most of all, **play it fair**!

KEEP GOING!!!

52
SAVED

No one is coming to save you.

I know this may be a hard pill to swallow, especially if you are in a situation that is stressful right now.

It is the truth and you must know it.

No one is coming.

You must save yourself.

I always tried to show up for others in ways that I wanted others to show up for me.

Sometimes they did and other times they didn't.

I am grateful for those who have helped me along my path and grateful for those who didn't help me.

I was looking for a savior and in doing so, I developed a need to be a savior for others.

If I could show up for someone else then I could prove that I was worthy somehow.

I was certain that if I showed up for others, that someone would show up for me.

It took time, heartbreak, frustration and some tough moments but eventually I got the message.

The message was that no one was coming to save me.

I had to save myself.

When I started showing up for myself and stopped worrying so much about showing up for others, my life changed.

What you must understand is that sometimes the people you believe GOD sent to help you were actually not assigned to help you but to teach you that you were always capable of helping yourself.

When you get tired of letting people use you, then you start to know what it means to surrender to purpose.

You experience the joy that comes with leaning into your gifts and allowing GOD to use you.

Believe in yourself and believe in your purpose.

You are powerful.

You are capable.

You are gifted.

Pour into yourself.

Help yourself and then help someone else.

Save yourself.

KEEP GOING!!!

53
A SONG FOR YOU

Dearest Dreamer,

I was listening to *A Song for You* by Donny Hathaway.

It is a mesmerizing song that reminds me of the beauty found in life's dark moments.

The first time I heard the song was on my uncle's iPod.

I was washing dishes recently when the song came on, and for the first time, the lyrics resonated in a different way.

My own journey helped me develop an appreciation for the darkness that comes with this experience we call life.

As I continued to reflect on the lyrics, I thought of what the words meant to me.

"Now I'm so much better, and if my words don't come together, listen to the melody, 'cause my love is in there hiding."

We're all fighting a battle that no one else knows about.

Kindness is a gift we should give ourselves and others.

When is the last time you showed gratitude (for yourself) for the hard work you have done?

When is the last time you took a moment to appreciate how far you have come?

When is the last time you were kind to yourself?

When is the last time you showed kindness to someone else?

This hasn't been an easy assignment.

I know that there have been times where the journey felt like Hell.

Sometimes it can be hard to differentiate between the song you are singing to yourself and the noise and chatter that comes from the outside world.

If you are not careful, the outside noise will start to sound like your song and your song will sound more like the outside noise.

The way you live your life will determine the music you make and the song you sing.

Sometimes the music doesn't always sound good but don't let that stop you from singing your song.

Remember that practice makes perfect.

Continue along your path with faith and determination.

When things get tough, Dreamer, listen for the melody of the music of life.

It is, in fact, where love is hiding.

Even the things that don't work out for you, work out for you in the end.

Everything is working for your good.

Sing your song, Dreamer.

Tell your story and inspire others.

KEEP GOING!!!

54
IF YOUR BOUNDARY...

Dearest Dreamer,

Along your path, you will experience trials and you will overcome them.

Stand in your faith.

You will meet people, love them deeply, and they will hurt you.

Stand in love.

You will hurt people on the path to your promise.

Stand in self-awareness.

You will offend some and harm others with your words.

Stand in compassion.

All of these things will happen and you will learn a lot about people and about yourself.

You will learn about boundaries.

You will learn how to set boundaries and how to respect them.

In the beginning it will be hard to set boundaries because you are not use to it.

In the past, you have always cut people off and moved on with your life, carrying the weight of your unshared feelings with you.

Things that could have been solved with a conversation, turned into missed opportunities to communicate, to forgive, and to be forgiven.

Could this experience have been avoided by setting a boundary?

I've always struggled with setting and enforcing my boundaries.

I was a pushover and a people pleaser.

I was a chronic bridge burner too, when a boundary probably would have corrected the issue.

You live and you learn, right?

As I grew more comfortable operating in my authenticity, the practice of setting boundaries became easier.

There were times where I set a boundary in order to save a bridge and it resulted in the other person making the decision to burn the bridge instead.

Other times, the bridge burning was a natural occurrence after a boundary had been set or needed to be enforced.

These moments of separation are necessary.

When your boundary burns a bridge, it is a blessing.

Keep setting your boundaries.

Keep being authentic.

Keep your faith.

KEEP GOING!!!

55
ALREADY

Dearest Dreamer,

Like many others before you, you will fall for a few tricks.

You will get caught up in what the world thinks about you and focus your time and energy on becoming that person.

At some point you will join the rat race.

Eventually, you will escape that fruitless pursuit, only to find yourself caught up in the same cycle as you navigate the path of entrepreneurship.

You want to, but you can't seem to shake the hold that *survival mode* has on you.

Can't you see how incredible you are?

Don't you see how brilliant you are?

Define your own success and don't wait for validation from others.

You are a trailblazer, Dreamer, so continue to be courageous and blaze a trail for the generations coming behind you.

Go forward with a bold faith and with gratitude.

Understand that you are already the thing you believe you are becoming.

Believe that everything you need in this moment, Dreamer, is already done; that is has already been given to you.

When you took that first step in faith, the end was already written.

Build with the understanding that what you are building is great already.

Now is not the time to quit.

Don't you get it?

You have **already won!**

All you have to do is **KEEP GOING!!!**

56
P.U.S.H.

P – PERSEVERE (PRAY)

U – Uplift (Until)

S – Shine (Something)

H – Heal (Happens)

Dearest Dreamer,
Continue to persevere.

Pray.

What is prayer?

Neale Donald Walsch wrote in *Conversations with GOD* that *"every thought you hold on to is a prayer."*

If every thought you hold on to is a prayer, then **hold on to the thought of your success**.

Hold on to thoughts of gratitude.

Hold on to your vision.

Hold on to your faith.

Uplift others until your season arrives.

Be humble enough to clap for others, understanding that your time is coming.

Don't envy the success of others.

You don't know the hell that they had to endure in order to align with their purpose.

Shine because there's something about your light that inspires others.

Shine because your light, like you, is a unique expression. There is no other light like yours, and whether you know it or not, you are an inspiration to many!

Keep shining.

Believe that healing happens.

You may be hurting right now, but trouble won't last always.

Your day will come and you will remember these difficult times and be grateful for them.

These are the moments that ground you in your purpose.

They make you grateful and ensure that you don't take your blessings for granted.

You have come this far, Dreamer.

Don't give up!

You are almost there.

Continue to PUSH.

KEEP GOING!!!

57
OBEDIENCE IS BETTER

Dearest Dreamer,

Obedience is better than sacrifice because obedience requires patience.

Impatience often leads to misalignment.

There will be many instances where you will find yourself out of alignment with your assignment.

You will use your gifts to benefit others.

You will continue to pour from an empty cup and live in frustration while you wait for help that isn't coming.

You will wonder why it seems like everything in your life is at a stand-still.

Maybe things are stagnant because you are not aligned with your path and your purpose.

You received the signs of confirmation that you asked for, Dreamer.

Be obedient and move.

Once you start moving, don't stop.

Never give up.

There will be times where what you are doing will not make sense to other people.

Guess what?

It isn't any of their business.

You have your orders, Dreamer.

Your mission awaits.

It is time for you to move…**so move**.

Your success is on the other side of your fear.

KEEP GOING!!!

58
BIGGER

Dearest Dreamer,

You are gaining some traction and things are going well!

Congratulations!

Take it all in and show gratitude for this moment.

You have worked hard and you deserve to bask in the light of your victory.

There is one thing that you have to remember, Dreamer.

Your purpose, is bigger than you.

It has always been bigger than you.

You are winning.

You are going to keep winning.

Stay humble.

Remember what the success is really for and why you have been put in position.

Don't lose your head.

Don't forget to leave a trail for the next person to follow and create opportunities for others when you can.

Plant seeds so that the next generation can reap the fruits.

Your purpose is rooted in people and bigger than politics.

Don't let the journey make you bitter.

Don't let the wins carry you away.

Stay grounded and remember the struggles and lessons you encountered along your path.

KEEP GOING!!!

59
DON'T MOVE MY MOUNTAINS

Dearest Dreamer,

When you asked for the assignment, you asked for the mountain too.

There will be times when you are climbing that mountain and you will pray to be released from the hardships that come with the climb.

In those moments, remember what the old song by Inez Andrews says…

"Lord, don't move my mountain but give me the strength to climb…"

Instead of asking for an easy way out, **ask for the strength to keep going.**

Pray for the faith to endure, and over time the mountain will *move you.*

You have come this far, Dreamer, don't stop now.

KEEP GOING!!!

60

LUCK REQUIRES

Dearest Dreamer,

Falling into the *luck trap* can be dangerous.

Choose faith over luck.

Luck requires no effort, no faith and makes no mention of GOD.

It is true that faith requires more work but when it is all said and done, there will be no denying that GOD's hand was in the process and every inch of ground that you gained was earned.

Luck takes for granted that you will be in the right place at the right time.

Faith gives you the strength to keep going even when your timing is off or you are in the *wrong* place.

I know it may be dark right now but you have something better than luck, Dreamer.

You have a vision.

You also have the faith needed to stick to your path and the patience that your promise requires.

Now is not the time to throw in the towel.

You are ready.

KEEP GOING!!!

61

THE WAY THROUGH

Dearest Dreamer,

It will get dark at times, but no matter how dark it gets, believe that you will make it to the other side of that dark moment.

When you make it out of Hell, Dreamer, don't let it go to your head.

Remember it was GOD's grace that carried you through those dark times.

Never forget that it was your faith that sustained you.

Make sure that you don't carry weight of bitterness, resentment and fear out of Hell with you.

You walked through the darkness of Hell so that you could re-discover your light.

You walked through Hell so that you could show others how to navigate the dark moments in their lives and make it to the other side of the experiences that they believe are meant to destroy them.

You walked through the shadows of Hell so that you could make others aware of their own light.

You made it to the other side to tell somebody else that they could make it too.

That is why you can't give up, Dreamer.

You were meant to show others the way.

You are a **Way-Shower**.

You can't quit.

Keep moving, Dreamer.

Remember, you are not just doing this for you.

The collective is waiting for you.

The world needs you in it.

The world needs your light!

KEEP GOING!!!

62

RECIPROCITY REQUIRES

Dearest Dreamer,

I was reflecting this morning about all of the *"gems"* I have given away over the years, in life and in business.

I was an over-giver by nature.

Notice I said, I was an *OVER-giver* and not just a regular giver.

I always gave at the expense of myself and most of the time, I was pouring from an empty cup.

There is nothing wrong with being a giver but over-giving often leads to disappointment and indicates a lack of self-worth.

It comes from this driving desperation to experience reciprocity in its fullness.

The truth is that some of the people you help will not be able to help you in return, and some will not have the desire.

Rest assured that the good you put into the world will come back to you.

Continue to do good and be good.

Start with yourself and extend the love to others.

I over-gave because I thought that it made me valuable.

I was wrong.

It did the opposite and I only ended up hurting myself.

You might find yourself in a place right now, Dreamer, where you have over-given and are stuck in a cycle of pouring from an empty cup.

You are depleted.

You are tired.

You don't trust people, and you have a tendency to believe that every situation is destined to result in a demonstration of *Murphy's Law*: *You believe that anything that can go wrong will go wrong.*

You continue to pour from an empty cup, in a frustrated attempt to showcase your *seemingly boundless* capacity to pour into others.

What is left over are the fruits that a *lack of self-love produces* – <u>NOTHING</u>!

You've given so much to so many people and you can count on one hand the number of people who poured into you.

You were keeping score?

Noted.

Here's the thing, Dreamer; **Reciprocity requires nothing.**

It is a universal law.

What you put out is what comes back to you.

What you give, is given unto you.

Trust that whenever you give from a place of love instead of lack, you are already blessed.

When you give to yourself first, you have filled your cup.

When you give to another, you have helped to fill theirs.

If they don't pour back into you, assume that their cup was not full enough to do so and hope that they will help another one day and *pay it forward*.

Let your giving be a reflection of the love that you have for yourself.

Before you can give the shirt off your back, you must first have a shirt.

In other words, stop pouring from a broken cup. Stop giving from an un-healed place.

Your reaping season is coming.

Now is not the time to lose your head, Dreamer.

Maintain your focus and continue pouring into yourself and filling your cup.

KEEP GOING!!!

63
PURPOSE. VISION. ACTION.

Dearest Dreamer,

Whatever you do, do it with purpose.

Your strength and resilience are inspiring. Continue to be driven by your purpose.

Your purpose is clear and your impact will be felt.

Lean into your gifts.

Understand that *vision is the essence of imagination.*

This is the reason that many others will not be able to see your vision.

Don't let that stop you.

Some will only be able to see the apple seed, while you possess the ability to see the tree, and the fruit that the tree will one day bear.

Others don't have to understand your vision.

Remember that GOD gave it to you.

They may not see it now but trust me, they will.

Hustling is no longer the name of the game.

It doesn't matter how many hours you work if you are working against yourself and going in a direction that is opposite the path you say you want to take.

There are two key words that will make your journey a lot more enjoyable or at least less stressful; *gratitude* and *alignment*.

Find gratitude for something, great or small, especially in the darkest and lowest moments of your life.

It is the first step toward inspiration and joy.

Alignment is part planning, part faith, part surrender and part *action*.

Align yourself with your purpose.

Align yourself with your vision.

Continue to take inspired action towards your dreams.

KEEP GOING!!!

64

BETWEEN

Dearest Dreamer,

At your best, you are selfish.

At your worst, you are altruistic.

At your most optimum, you exist in harmony and balance between the two.

Be selfish – **fill your own cup first**.

Be altruistic – **give without expecting anything in return.**

You will find balance between the two when you learn to allow others to drink from your saucer, all of the blessings that overflow from your cup, and reserve the contents in your cup for yourself.

You cannot help others if you can't help yourself.

Remember that the balance is always found *somewhere between*.

KEEP GOING!!!

65
INSPIRED BY LIGHT

Dearest Dreamer,

I was reflecting on what makes our light so inspiring.

Is it the darkness that we must go through to realize the full power of our light?

Has the light always been this powerful and vibrant and we only realize it after experiencing dark times?

I didn't develop an appreciation for my own light until I saw that it had the ability to inspire others even in moments when I myself was not inspired.

I was inspired by the encounters with others and quickly came to realization that inspiration, like laughter, is contagious.

You have inspired more people than you will ever know, Dreamer.

Your light is brilliant.

It is powerful.

It is needed at this time.

It may be dark right now, Dreamer, but it won't be dark much longer.

Use your light to illuminate your path.

You are almost there.

KEEP GOING!!!

66

WAITING TO ARRIVE

Dearest Dreamer,

If you wait for your moment to arrive, you will always be late.

I spent so much time waiting for a moment that didn't come.

Don't fall into the same trap.

Like the old saying goes: "If *you live for their applause, then you'll die by their boos.*"

This journey, for me, has been about grounding myself in who I truly am and finding my center.

I was waiting to publish these letters.

I thought no one would listen to me unless I had some sort of success that could be seen by others.

I realize now that it was not up to me to amplify the message. All I needed to do was continue to do the work and be obedient.

Be obedient and trust that GOD will do the amplifying.

Open your mouth and GOD will speak for you.

Truth doesn't need a stage and lights.

It doesn't need a microphone; **it stands on its own and will amplify itself.**

Truth doesn't even need anyone to believe it.

It simply exists.

The truth is that you were made to inspire, uplift, and heal others.

Your story will inspire someone.

Don't wait for your moment to arrive.

Be in the moment and make the most of it.

Your moment is NOW!

Show up.

Be grateful.

Don't be so focused on the moments that didn't go *according to plan,* that you miss the lessons that the experiences were meant to teach you.

Remember that this journey is a marathon and not a sprint, Dreamer.

Stay focused.

Stay inspired.

KEEP GOING!!!

67
YOU DON'T KNOW

Dearest Dreamer,

I know that the weight of your promise can feel like a burden.

You have been fighting so hard and it feels like all of your hard work was in vain.

You have nothing to show for it.

You don't know if the direction you are currently going in, is the right direction.

Are you really called to do this or is this just something that you would like to do?

What if the weight of your brokenness that is holding you back?

What if the weight of your bitterness is holding you back?

What if the weight of your disappointment is holding you back?

This is a long journey and you are going to face hardships.

Don't let past failures hold you back and discourage you from trying again.

Sometimes you don't know and sometimes that's the point.

Not knowing, will require you to stand in your faith.

It will require that you cut out all of the noise and learn to go within.

You don't know what is coming next, but what you *do know* is that you have reached a stage in your journey where it is between you and GOD.

Trust the process.

You don't know if you have the stamina to last in this race much longer but what you do know is that you have come too far to turn back.

KEEP GOING!!!

68

SHADOW GAMES

Dearest Dreamer,

It took me a long time to find the balance between my light and my shadow.

My light is a gift to the world.

My shadow is a gift to myself.

Don't favor one over the other because they are meant to work together.

Appreciate the fullness of who you are.

Do your best to do the work and heal from your past traumas and experiences; that old hurt is what your shadow likes to feed on.

Remember that you always have the power to choose.

Keep your eyes, heart, and mind open.

Embrace your light.

Embrace your shadow.

Together they make up the fullness of your power.

KEEP GOING!!!

69
FAKE IT

Dearest Dreamer,

You know most of this is fake, right?

It is all smoke and mirrors.

One day, you will experience the money, the power, and all the trappings that come with wealth and success.

At some point you will discover that those things are empty and hollow.

Most people are focused on the wrong things and don't even realize it.

I didn't understand how powerful the impact of my early failures and setbacks was until I began to walk by faith, hand in hand with GOD on the path to my promise.

Wisdom is discovered in your failures, struggles, and setbacks.

Understanding is found in your experiences if you take the time to reflect and gain understanding.

Remember that the breaking is *necessary*.

You can't fake the breaking process.

The olive must be pressed in order to get the oil.

There is no oil without pressing.

Pressing is breaking and breaking is pressing.

The diamond cannot be formed without the pressing and the breaking.

There is purpose in the pressing and the breaking.

It is meant to strengthen you and to prepare you to carry the weight of your promise.

Don't fake it, FEEL IT.

Live it.

See it.

BELIEVE IT and **KEEP GOING!!!**

70
LIFE IS A CANVAS

Dearest Dreamer,

Life is a canvas, and its experiences are the colors with which we paint.

Don't give up before your masterpiece is complete.

KEEP GOING!!!

71
THIS TOO...

Dearest Dreamer,

I know it feels like life has you in a headlock right now.

I know that the walls feel like they are closing in on you.

You have been through a lot.

You have continued to endure and through faith you have persevered.

Do you remember the moment when things were at their lowest?

You made it to the other side of that moment.

You overcame the obstacle.

You will experience dark moments again.

<u>**Remember that it is only a moment, and like every moment before, this moment too, shall pass.**</u>

Rest in gratitude and continue to do the work.

KEEP GOING!!!

72
ANOTHER LITTLE PIECE OF
MY HEART

Dearest Dreamer,

You have given away so much of yourself to others.

Physically.

Mentally.

Spiritually.

Emotionally.

Spending time with yourself has taught you that your presence is a gift.

Your vibe, your energy, it is a blessing.

You sharing your energy in an open, genuine and authentic way, is a blessing; first to yourself and then to others.

It is a gift to yourself first because you honor yourself when you operate in your authenticity.

It is a gift to others when they are inspired by your authenticity.

You are blessing others when you are open.

You are blessing others when you share your love, your energy, and your light.

Everyone shouldn't have access to you, so you will need to learn to be selective with the company that you keep.

Allow time, energy, and truth to guide you as you navigate the relationships closest to you.

You won't always get things right and in those moments when you don't, forgive yourself, ask for forgiveness from others, and work to make amends.

Continue to share your gifts.

Every time you share your gifts, you share a piece of your heart and bare a piece of your soul.

Beware not to give yourself away, Dreamer.

It is up to you to protect your gift and your space.

Be unapologetically vigilant and don't let up on your boundaries.

Continue to do the work.

Learn the lessons.

Apply the knowledge.

Live the wisdom.

KEEP GOING!!!

73
FROM MY SAUCER

Dearest Dreamer,

The lesson that I am about to share with you took me many years to learn.

I am not sure when it started for me but I do remember that I became a people pleaser very early in my life.

As a child, I was usually the odd ball and it felt like no one passed up on an opportunity to remind me that I was the odd ball.

This resulted in me wanting to be accepted.

I have always been a giver and eventually my giving evolved into _over-giving_.

I understand now that my lack of self-worth made me an over-giver.

I gave *myself* away.

I gave *my gifts* away.

I gave *my time* away.

I gave *my energy* away.

Eventually, I was left empty and bitter.

This letter is inspired by a poem that I read once.

I believe that it's called *"Drinking from My Saucer."*

My Gran found it years ago and shared it with the family. It has stuck with me over the years.

In the poem, the writer focuses on **gratitude** as a theme and ends each verse with the same line.

"I am drinking from my saucer because my cup has overflowed..."

A few years ago, this poem found its way back to me at a time when I really needed it.

My experiences had given me a greater appreciation for the poem and its meaning.

I still felt gratitude for the experiences but I also understood what it was like to pour from an empty cup and the emptiness that results from pouring from an empty cup.

I learned to let GOD fill my cup and not to expect my blessings to come from the people to whom I had been a blessing.

Eventually, I was freed from the burden of over-giving.

My cup is for me and so are the blessings that GOD pours into my cup.

You can't pour from an empty cup, Dreamer.

Remember that the blessings in your cup are for you.

Continue to allow GOD to fill your cup.

Be selfish.

You can't help another until you have helped yourself.

One day, you will look up and realize, with gratitude, that your cup is overflowing.

Do not fall back into the trap of over-giving.

Let others drink from your saucer.

Help others but not at the expense of yourself.

KEEP GOING!!!

74

ALL THE ANTS

Dearest Dreamer,

You know by now (or maybe you don't) that this journey comes with its ups and downs.

You will meet a lot of people on your path and many of those relationships will be short-lived.

Don't panic; it is all a part of your process.

There may be some instances where your free will or the free will of another will alter the dynamics of the relationships closest to you.

Trust the process.

Some people you meet along the way will not have the best intentions for you.

Don't take it personal, Dreamer.

They will smile in your face and talk about you behind your back.

Let them talk and stay focused on your vision.

They will never truly know all that you have overcome to make it this far.

Don't waste your time and energy seeking revenge or trying to prove yourself to them.

If you do the work, your absence and continued success will speak for you.

The truth is that you won't need revenge.

Eventually, you won't even remember what caused the separation in the first place, but it will be clear that a separation has occurred.

What will be more clear is that the separation was necessary.

Stay focused, Dreamer.

You can't crush all the ants so don't waste your time and energy trying.

Let them be and keep your eyes on the prize.

KEEP GOING!!!

75
VAMPIRES

Dearest Dreamer,

Sometimes you can be *too open*.

There is nothing wrong with being open, but you don't want to be *too open*.

You must protect your space and your energy from those who may not have your best interests at heart.

Watch out for the *Energy Vampires*.

Energy Vampires will smell you coming from a mile away, Dreamer.

They will latch onto you and drain your energy.

Be careful with these people.

When dealing with them, it is important to set boundaries and to know your worth.

Do the work so that you can discover and experience a relationship with yourself that is balanced.

Build a forcefield of joy and peace around you, and be aware of any shifts that take place in your *force*.

In the Bible, when the woman with the issue of blood touched the hem of Jesus' robe, He knew and asked immediately touched Him?

The woman didn't get close enough to touch Him physically but He still felt someone enter his space.

He felt the disturbance in *his forcefield*.

What strikes me about the story is the fact that Jesus was so in tune with his own vibration that he immediately became aware of the fact that an energy that wasn't his own was pulling on Him.

The woman with the issue, found herself in a low place due to her circumstances.

In other words, her circumstances caused her to be in a low place; it didn't mean that she was a bad person.

You know what it is to find yourself in a low place, Dreamer.

It is a humbling experience.

I believe that her experience of this lower vibration was a blessing because it is the very thing that drove her to seek healing.

It did not stop her from seeking the help that she needed.

It did not stop her from healing.

I can identify with the woman.

I know the work that it takes to heal and raise your vibration.

It is work that never stops.

If you do the work then you will sharpen your sensitivity and know when your equilibrium has been disrupted and *your force* has been disturbed.

You will know because you will feel it.

Use your discernment when dealing with others.

Your gut will never lie to you but your mind and heart can convince you not to listen to your gut.

Jesus didn't have to touch or even turn his attention to the woman in order to heal her; all she had to do was touch the hem of his garment.

She entered his energy field, his vibration, and was immediately healed by it.

Your energy is healing.

Your light is powerful, Dreamer.

Your light has the power to heal and this will attract all sorts of people.

They will latch onto your light.

Pay attention.

Remember that a vampire is not allowed to enter your home or space unless you invite them in, so be careful whom you invite into your space, Dreamer.

Trust the process.

Everybody can't go with you, even the people you want to go with you the most.

You will outgrow some people as you go to your next level.

Don't let the good you believe you see in others keep you in dead situations.

Understand that sometimes the good you see in others is just a reflection of the good that exists within you.

Do the work, Dreamer.

Heal yourself.

Continue to do the work.

Watch out for the Energy Vampires.

Protect your space.

Protect your peace.

Protect your energy.

Protect your gifts.

Protect your joy.

Cut the ties that bind you and don't look back.

Choose yourself and prioritize your peace.

KEEP GOING!!!

76
BROKEN CRAYONS

Dearest Dreamer,

You are brilliant.

You are broken.

Remember that even broken crayons can still color.

KEEP GOING!!!

77
FROM MY WORTH AND NOT MY WOUND

DEAREST DREAMER,

I saw a post on Instagram years ago that said something about operating *from your worth and not your wound.*

This made me think of all the times that I made decisions from my wound instead of a sense of self-worth or love.

This is why doing the work is so important.

Don't skip the lessons.

The lessons will teach you that your worth is *__immeasurable__*.

You have chosen from your wound because you do not believe that you are worthy of more.

You know better now and now that you know your worth, choose from that space.

Choose *joy.*

Choose *healing*.

Choose *peace*.

Choose *love*.

Choose *YOU*.

KEEP GOING!!!

78
WASTED

Dearest Dreamer,

Understand that no experience is a waste.

Your life is not a waste.

I watched a powerful documentary on YouTube called _Shelter_.

It follows a group of people from various walks of life.

These are the types people that society tends to overlook.

I continued to watch the documentary and realized that I related to a lot of what some of the main subjects were experiencing in their lives.

I was reminded that I could have been in their shoes.

There was a brief moment where I thought about how I didn't want my life to be a waste.

I wanted to do something that would have a lasting impact.

I didn't want to waste my gifts or my talents but this didn't stop me from continuing to sit on my gifts and talents.

I passed judgement and discounted those people without a second thought.

GOD spoke to me in that moment and I was immediately convicted.

"Who said their lives were a waste? They are just as talented and as brilliant as you. You all are made from the same stuff. You are ONE."

The person who stood out to me the most was a young lady named Elizabeth.

She appeared to be a kind and gentle soul who bent in an effort to adjust to the pressures of life. It was clear that some parts of her experience had broken her but didn't completely destroy her.

I noticed that Elizabeth possessed an inner light that her life's circumstances could not break.

In one scene, Elizabeth is singing a song.

"What's love got to do with it?" she sings.

Her answer is the thing that struck me.

She pauses for a brief moment and replies, **EVERYTHING.**

As I continued to watch the documentary I grew more inspired.

The experiences that led Elizabeth and the other people in the film to that moment were not wasted because they inspired the documentary, which inspired me, and later became the inspiration for this letter.

Your experiences are not a waste, Dreamer, they all serve you in the pursuit of your promise.

Don't give up.

Don't let you past stop you.

Don't allow fear to get the best of you.

You story will be a source of inspiration.

It is not too late and you are more than your past mistakes.

KEEP GOING!!!

79
SILENCE IS SOMETIMES LOUD AND ALWAYS GOLDEN

Dearest Dreamer,

You will be overlooked.

You will be mistreated.

You will be used and abused.

Learn to control your emotions.

Learn to be observant and to practice patience.

Pay attention.

Allow silence to be your response to certain things and take notes.

Always remember that some things are only meant to be seen, heard, felt, and then noted.

Your silence will speak volumes.

Your silence will be LOUD.

Focus on the work and let the work speak for you.

Move in silence, Dreamer.

Build in silence.

Win in silence.

The world will hear you soon enough.

KEEP GOING!!!

80

JEALOUSY

Dearest Dreamer,

People will envy you and some will even be jealous of you.

Pay them no mind but don't be so oblivious that you don't pay them any attention at all.

Keep your eyes open.

Jealousy is mis-channeled inspiration.

Appreciate the fact that a hater is just a fan, living in a state of confusuion.

You inspire them so much; they don't know how to tell you, so they choose to hate you instead.

Don't waste your time and energy being jealous of others. You don't know the cost of their oil or the pressing process that they had to go through in order to create the oil that is the anointing on their life.

Jealously is a dangerous spirit, so don't take it lightly.

Beware of connecting with jealous energies who secretly hate you and don't want you to be successful.

They will drag you down and dim your light whenever they get the opportunity.

Remember not to overthink it, as jealousy is a part of life's experiences.

Don't take it personal.

If you are jealous of another person, you are not walking in or focused enough on your own purpose.

Walk in your authenticity and focus on living in your purpose and you will be so consumed by your path that you won't have time to be jealous of what others are doing.

Clap for others when they succeed; especially because you know the shared struggles that we all face on this journey.

Choose to be inspired by the accomplishments of others and appreciate them as a symbol of what is possible for you.

You moment is coming; until it does, **KEEP GOING!!!**

81

THE GENESIS OF CREATIVITY

Dearest Dreamer,

You have a vision.

Some people will think that you are crazy because your vision is so big.

They will attempt to make you feel silly, like what you see for yourself is impossible.

Let them think whatever they want.

Crazy **is the genesis of vision**.

Everything that manifests itself in this world, started with a vision.

<u>**You have to be a little crazy to pursue your promise.**</u>

You were crazy enough to believe in yourself.

<u>You were crazy enough to step out on faith.</u>

You were crazy enough to have faith that you would overcome the hardships, setbacks and failures you encountered on your path.

You were crazy enough to keep going.

It all starts with a crazy idea.

You are not crazy, Dreamer.

You are inspired.

KEEP GOING!!!

82

CHOSEN

Dearest Dreamer,

You are a *Chosen One* because **you chose yourself.**

You chose **the process.**

You chose to go **through the darkness.**

You chose to **shine your light.**

You chose to **look for your light in spite of your darkness.**

You chose to **find balance between your light and your darkness and now you see that the beauty in both.**

You chose to not give up on your dreams.

Remember that the choice is <u>yours</u>.

KEEP GOING!!!

83
EVEN IN FAILURE

Dearest Dreamer,

If you think that you are going to move along your path without experiencing failure, you are sadly mistaken.

Do you believe that failure is final?

It is not.

Failure is simply a part of the process.

Even in your failure, you will find success if you learn from and apply the lessons that the failure is meant to teach you.

Look beyond the failure for the lesson and **take only those things that serve you from the experience, leaving the rest to simply be A PART OF THE EXPERIENCE.**

You only fail if you quit.

As long as you don't quit, you will be successful, even in moments when you believe that you are failing.

Don't give up!

KEEP GOING!!!

84

THE FINAL VERDICT

Dearest Dreamer,

Each experience is a loss, a lesson, or both.

The final verdict will be determined by your perspective and how you see the experience.

Do you believe that these things are happening *to you* or *for you*?

If you really believe that all things work for your good, then you should never fear rejection or failure of any kind.

Remember that rejection is GOD's protection.

How many of those *"no's"* opened new doors for you?

Didn't some of those *"goodbyes"* save your life?

<u>What is for you, will always make its way to you.</u>

Trust the plan and know that there is a bigger picture and a grander story being written.

The final verdict is all about how you see things.

Where others see failure, you see victory.

Where others see loss, you see process.

The final verdict is _**VICTORY**_.

KEEP GOING!!!

85
FOR YOUR GOOD

Dearest Dreamer,

Whatever is happening in your life right now, believe that it is happening for your good.

Be grateful for the lessons.

Be grateful for each moment.

Believe that everything is working for your good.

Life is working for you and not against you.

Continue to walk by faith and not by sight.

Your time will come.

KEEP GOING!!!

86

FORGIVENESS

DEAREST DREAMER,

In this life, you will interact with people who won't *do right* by you.

If you are operating in your authenticity, then you are willing to admit that there are a fair share of people whom you have mistreated throughout your journey.

The key to learning the difficult lessons that come with these experiences is found in forgiveness and in forgiving yourself.

Self-awareness is what allows you to understand that sometimes you will hurt people, even when you don't mean to do it.

Forgive yourself; take the lesson and move on.

Don't take anything personally; that is a great way to waste your time and energy.

I was told once that I would not be able to do the work that I wanted to do unless I got a degree or some sort of certification.

Although neither of these things was required for me to do the work that I was doing, I was told that it would help to make the potential clients more comfortable with working with me.

It was a painful experience at the time because I wanted the project s0 badly.

The experience turned out to be a blessing in disguise, in many ways.

I was bitter about the experience for a long time, carrying feelings of resentment long after proving the person who said it wrong.

Being hurt and operating from that space made it easier to hold onto the anger.

Heal the hurt and diminish the anger.

That experience was necessary.

It was a part of my process.

It was also an opportunity to dig deeper and explore my true feelings.

Once I did the work that my healing required, I was able to see things from a new vantage point.

Perhaps they didn't mean any harm, and the experience was really an opportunity for me to focus more on developing my creative gifts and leaning into my calling.

Don't let the negative experiences break you.

The obstacles were never meant to stop you.

Those moments of resistance are meant to redirect you or give you the opportunity to see things from a different perspective.

I didn't allow the negative experiences to stop me.

Don't allow your disappointments and setbacks to stop you, Dreamer.

Look at how far you have come.

Apply what you have learned and don't give up.

Forgive and learn to be forgiven.

Start with yourself, and extend that same love and grace to others.

KEEP GOING!!!

87
THEY WILL SEE

Dearest Dreamer,

You have spent enough time talking.

You have spent enough time trying to prove yourself to others.

You have wasted enough time trying to prove others wrong.

Focus your energy instead on building, and forget the rest; it is only noise, a distraction meant to lure you away from your path.

When I first started my business, I felt the need to tell everyone what my next move was going to be.

I wanted to be seen.

I wanted to be heard.

I wanted respect, and most of all, I wanted power.

Of course, *I wanted money too.*

I was driven by ego and had no problem faking it until I made it.

It was an exhausting experience.

Dreamer, remember that you do not have anything to prove.

Don't you know that?

You do not need to be understood by others.

Walk in your purpose.

Maintain a clear vision and don't pay attention to the naysayers.

When you feel lost or overwhelmed with darkness, remember to go within.

Shine your light.

Remember that you don't walk alone on this path.

**GOD is with you*!*

Remember that there is no need to say what others will eventually see.

Let your work speak for you.

KEEP GOING!!!

88

I AM

Dearest Dreamer,

I am **nothing**.

I am **everything**.

I am **anything**.

I am a **moment**.

You are <u>**capable**</u>.

You are <u>**strong**</u>.

You are <u>**powerful**</u>.

You are <u>**connected**</u>.

You are <u>**protected**</u>.

You are <u>**called**</u>.

You are **gifted**.

<u>**GOD's grace is sufficient and made perfect in weakness.**</u>

Go forward boldly and fulfill your destiny, Dreamer.

**Allow your gifts to make room for you.**

Be open and allow the good you do for others to return to you.

You _WILL_ be victorious!

Remember who you are.

KEEP GOING!!!

89
THE OVERWHELMING
WEIGHT OF VISION

Dearest Dreamer,

When you decided to take that first leap of faith, you accomplished more than most people.

<u>You found the courage to take the first step.</u>

Do not forget to celebrate yourself and your wins, big or small.

Remember that some people never even start because the weight of their vision and the fear that comes with it paralyzes them.

<u>*You chose to step out on faith despite the weight and hardships that came with your journey.*</u>

You carry it well, Dreamer.

Don't quit.

Be encouraged and **KEEP GOING!!!**

90
A TEAM FOR TIRED ARMS

Dearest Dreamer,

You cannot build your vision alone.

Sometimes in my desperation to have a *"team"*, I would accept anyone who was willing to help, even if there were signs that we were not aligned.

What you need in order to build your vision, is going to take more than just any team, Dreamer.

The team you need is one for *tired arms*.

I got this concept from a story that I read years ago in the Bible.

In Exodus, Chapter 17, Moses realizes that he must hold up his arms while Joshua and the Israelites battle The Amalekites.

He goes to the top of a hill with Aaron and Hur to watch the battle.

As long as Moses held up his arms, Joshua and the Israelites were victorious and maintained a strong advantage on the battlefield.

I imagine that Moses probably started out strong, a lot like you did when you started on your journey.

His arms weren't tired in the beginning and neither were yours.

The battle is a long one, Dreamer.

When his arms got tired, Moses lowered them, and as a result, Joshua and the army started to lose their dominance over the Amalekites.

Aaron and Hur noticed this and put a stone under Moses for him to sit. Then each of them took one of Moses' arms and held it up *FOR HIM* and as a result, the Israelites defeated the Amalekites in battle.

Be grateful for those who support you along your path.

After the battle was won, Moses' father-in-law, Jethro, came to visit him along with Moses' wife and two children.

Upon observing Moses in his official capacity, Jethro advised him that the way Moses was managing things was not sustainable.

He told Moses that he needed to set up a team and then a system that would help him manage the workload, and help to preserve his energy.

Moses listened to his father-in-law and put a team and system in place, and it was a success.

Remember to build a team of people around you who will hold up your arms and will never remind you that they held them for you when you grew tired.

<u>Rid yourself of those who would remind you, after the battle is won, that they are the reason for your success.</u>

Your team will reveal itself as you continue along your path, Dreamer.

Remember, it only took two people to support Moses in order for the Israelites to be victorious in battle.

Until your team is complete, rely on GOD to hold you up when you get tired on this journey.

You started with a purpose.

You are on a mission, Dreamer.

It is not easy and it was not supposed to be.

Embrace the battle and be grateful for the support.

You will be victorious.

KEEP GOING!!!

91
THE TRUTH THAT INTRODUCES

Dearest Dreamer,

Keep your heart pure and maintain clear boundaries.

You will meet many people on the path to your promise.

You will think you know some of them and be surprised by the actions of others.

When the truth introduces you, remember that it was never personal.

Accept it for what it is and move forward with love and gratitude for the lesson and the experience.

It reminds me of one of my favorite lines from a song by Nipsey Hussle called *Bigger Than Life,* where Nipsey says,

"The world would not know Jesus Christ if there was never Judas. This knife that's in my back will be the truth that introduced us, and the distance in between us, is the proof of my conclusion."

I have discovered that two things are true when it comes to these experiences;

(1) Your hardships have the power to bless you and others if you don't give up.

(2) Instead of being bitter about the experiences, find gratitude for each of them.

Be grateful for each person you encounter along your path.

They taught you a valuable lesson and, in the end, the lesson is a blessing.

It was never personal.

In those low moments, find a way to transmute the hurt and convert that pain into humility and power.

Discover the peace that comes with acceptance and be grateful for it.

Conserve your energy, Dreamer, and maintain your focus.

Continue to put one foot in front of the other and move forward with faith.

When they show you who they are, believe them. (Maya Angelou)

Give them grace and send them on their way with love.

Don't let anything stop you from completing the mission.

KEEP GOING!!!

92
PATIENCE

DEAREST DREAMER,

Patience is both a virtue and a requirement to live in the fullness of your promise.

Anything that comes to you with ease (with the exception of your gift) is either a trap, a lesson, or both.

You can avoid a lot of mistakes by using your discernment.

There will be some other pitfalls that will are unavoidable along your path.

Patience is trusting in a divine plan that you didn't write and don't remember, while also understanding, believing, and accepting that the details of that plan were already written on your heart long before you got here.

Your path is destined, Dreamer.

Patience is less about waiting and more about trusting.

Your promise requires patience.

It requires perseverance.

It requires grit and tenacity.

It requires steadfast determination.

It requires faith.

It requires you to be patient with yourself and the process.

Trust that your promise is part of a divine plan and that your journey is the blueprint that will inspire someone else as they pursue their promise.

Your story has the power to sustain others on their journey.

Remember that there is no destination and the journey unfolds for you as you continue along your path.

KEEP GOING!!!

93
THE MESSAGE

Dearest Dreamer,

You are frustrated.

You are tired.

You are disillusioned.

You have been putting all that you have into what you are doing and you don't see any of the results you expected.

It feels like life is kicking you around for no reason.

You feel unworthy.

You feel that you have a message and no one is listening.

Perhaps the message doesn't lie in your words.

Maybe the message lies in the *JOURNEY*.

I was meditating one day, reflecting on my own journey.

I reflected on how grateful I was for the journey and the experiences that taught me such valuable lessons.

These letters are a part of my message.

I am allowing others to see what GOD is doing in my life, with my life, and through my life, using these letters.

They are a part of my story.

How will you share your story, Dreamer?

How will you ensure that your experiences (good or bad) are a source of inspiration for others?

Remember that your experiences have power.

Your story has power.

<u>Your story _is_ the message.</u>

Tell your story.

KEEP GOING!!!

94
MIND WARS

Dearest Dreamer,

The only war that matters is the one that you are fighting in your own mind.

Anything else is simply a distraction.

Do not get distracted, Dreamer.

<u>Pay attention.</u>

I started a podcast back in 2020, during the pandemic, called *A Loner's Guide to the Galaxy*.

It became a sacred space for me to express myself.

The Galaxy that I refer to in the podcasts is a space that exists for all of us to explore; it is in our minds.

I can remember a few times where that battle was almost lost.

You know what it is to fight those thoughts in your mind that hold you back and distract you from your purpose.

We are all fighting a war in our minds that no one else knows about.

Find ways to quiet your mind, Dreamer.

Once you discover peace, let nothing disrupt it.

To know GOD is to experience the fullness of JOY.

To know yourself is to know **GOD**.

To experience genuine goodness in the world around you is proof that **GOD is real**.

To be the one who creates an opportunity for another to experience genuine goodness is a blessing; it is GOD in action.

Right now, you may feel defeated but remember that you are destined to win this war!

It was already written.

This war is a part of your destiny and every battle you fight is rooted in your purpose and preparing you on the path to your promise.

Remember to take each battle as it comes to you and that not all battles need to be fought.

No matter what, don't give up.

KEEP GOING!!!

95
BLIND LOYALTY

Dearest Dreamer,

Loyalty is important but don't value loyalty over respect.

Blind loyalty is dangerous.

It will inspire you to help another push a car that has run out of gas up a hill.

You will continue to struggle and push, exhausting yourself in the process.

You keep pushing; your loyalty driving you to show up for others at the expense of yourself.

<u>Use your discernment.</u>

Don't allow others to trick you into being blindly loyal to them.

<u>Remember that you will know them by the fruit that they bear.</u>

KEEP GOING!!!

96
THE GENIUS THAT TRAUMA CREATES

Dearest Dreamer,

No one gets through life without experiencing some level of trauma.

You have experienced your fair share of neglect, abuse, and other trauma that was meant to destroy you but didn't.

Your trauma will ignite your creative genius and create opportunities for you to use your gifts to heal yourself and others.

<u>Your trauma does not define you.</u>

It is your darkness that makes your light shine so bright.

Sharing your gifts is how you shine your light in this world.

Lean into your gifts and explore the full magnitude of your creative genius.

You are destined to do great things, Dreamer.

Do not let the darkness overtake you.

Remember that it is all working for your good.

KEEP GOING!!!

97
THE BLESSING OF PERSPECTIVE

Dearest Dreamer,

Your experiences help shape your perspective.

Understand that with time your perspective will change.

Be open to the possibilities this shift in perspective will bring.

When it comes to others and their perspective, don't take it personal.

They are only able to see the world through the lens of their own personal experiences.

Keep your focus, Dreamer and don't allow the chatter from others to sway you along your path.

Believe in the work that you are doing.

Continue to evolve your perspective and welcome the shift.

Embrace the blessing that is a changed and renewed mind.

If you do not like what you see, try to see things differently.

KEEP GOING!!!

98
YOU SAY...

Dearest Dreamer,

A couple of years ago while we were taking one of our evening walks, I was telling Stasha about a big opportunity that our firm had just secured.

It was an exciting time but I was also very anxious.

I was excited about the opportunity but the truth was that I didn't really enjoy doing the work that was required to complete the project successfully.

I was grateful that the project was a paid one and decided that I would show up and do my best.

I was telling Stasha about some of my thoughts and feelings surrounding the deal and the project.

I told her about all of the work and responsibility that came with the engagement and how I wasn't sure if I could handle it or not.

She listened patiently, like she always does, as we continued to walk.

She looked at me and asked,

"Why are you running backwards when you say you want to run forward? Take the parachute off."

It was her way of telling me to stop resisting and to lean into the opportunity that I had prayed for for so long.

It was exactly what I needed to hear in that moment.

Maybe you need to be reminded that you manifested this moment.

<u>You prayed for this opportunity.</u>

<u>Stop getting in your own way, Dreamer.</u>

Don't resist the changes happening in your life.

Take the parachute off and get rid of anything that slows you down or creates unnecessary resistance along your path.

As you get closer to your promise, you will have to make tough choices to cut ties with dead weight.

You say that you want to heal; **let go of past offenses**.

You say that you want peace; **let go of ego**.

You say you want joy; **create with love, intention and purpose.**

You say you want to make it; **KEEP GOING!!!**

99
NOAH DIDN'T KNOW

Dearest Dreamer,

Noah didn't know when the flood was coming.

He had faith and built the ark.

He *PREPARED*.

Noah trusted GOD and also believed in himself and his ability to build the thing that GOD inspired him to build.

He trusted in the process and knew that GOD would keep GOD's word.

He also had to believe in himself because GOD can give the assignment, but if we do not believe in our ability to complete the assignment, then the process cannot complete itself.

There will be times on your journey, Dreamer, where you will feel like Noah.

There will be moments where you feel like you are not making any progress.

Trust the process.

When the flood comes, you will be glad that you continued to build in spite of the obstacles.

One day the flood will come and all of the things that you once knew will be washed away and replaced, providing you with a clean slate.

Keep building, Dreamer.

Be faithful in your work because there is purpose in your pursuit.

There is purpose in the weight of your promise.

There is purpose in your pain.

You were made for this.

Keep believing.

Keep building!

The storm will come.

Prepare.

KEEP GOING!!!

100

THE COST OF A DREAM

Dearest Dreamer,

Attach yourself to nothing during your journey.

Things are constantly changing and you will be forced to adapt.

Expect that things will not go according to *your* plan and that everything is unfolding as a part of a *divine plan*.

Understand that your promise will not come without a cost.

Your dream will cost you something.

Are you willing to pay the cost, Dreamer?

The answer to that question is found in the work you do every day as you continue to pursue your promise.

Do not beg, steal or borrow to get to your promise.

You cannot take shortcuts.

Do the work!

The price of your dream should *NEVER* be your soul.

"What does it benefit a man to gain the world and lose his soul?"

Do not sell your soul, Dreamer.

KEEP GOING!!!

101

THE POWER OF YOUR PIVOT-MOMENT

Dearest Dreamer,

Never underestimate the power of a well-timed *pivot-moment*.

A *pivot-moment* is an opportunity for you to choose.

You can choose to see the problem or you can take action in your present moment to discover a solution to your problem.

You can start by seeing your problem as an opportunity.

When you make the decision to pivot, you are stepping out on faith.

It was a pivot moment that created the opportunity for me to finally complete these letters and finish developing this book.

You will learn to go with the flow in situations that you have no control over.

Trust that you are flowing in the right direction.

See the opportunity instead of the obstacle.

Pivot when you must but whatever you do, Dreamer, don't resist the opportunity to evolve.

KEEP GOING!!!

102

WHAT WAS AND WHAT WILL BE

Dearest Dreamer,

I was watching a video on YouTube from Queen Cup, a spiritual healer, messenger, tarot reader, spiritualist, and teacher that I have been watching on YouTube for a number of years.

In the video she was speaking about the changes that we all go through in life, especially the changes that come with personal growth and elevation.

As she was encouraging viewers to keep going, she said something that I thought was profound and I wanted to share it here.

She said, *"What was, is no more, and what will be, is beautiful."*

It reminded me that there is beauty in change.

In fact, change is the only constant in this life.

Everything is in a constant state of evolution and you are no different.

<u>You must learn to adapt.</u>

You must make adjustments and pivot when necessary.

Whether times are good or bad, one thing remains true: things will change.

You are not who you used to be, Dreamer.

You have evolved.

You have been reborn.

You have learned and incorporated the lessons from your experiences.

Keep evolving.

Keep dreaming.

Keep adapting.

KEEP GOING!!!

103
YEAR 33

Dearest Dreamer,

Today I turned thirty-three (33).

It is a blessing.

Another trip around the sun.

It is another opportunity to have impact.

Thank you, GOD, for my life.

Thank you for my gifts.

They make *room* for me.

They create *ROOMS* for me.

I am a vessel.

This year, I will do the thing that I was born to do.

<u>I will **write**.</u>

I will **write the letters**.

I will **shine my light.**

I will **love more.**

I will **live more.**

I will forgive more.

I will **learn to let go.**

I will **learn to embrace.**

I will learn balance.

I will **know peace and experience the fullness of joy.**

I will **KEEP GOING!!!**

104

DON'T SELL

Dearest Dreamer,

What is for you will not require you to sell yourself.

It will only require you to _BE YOURSELF_.

In order to free yourself, you must be yourself.

When you learn to embrace yourself, you will not care if you are accepted by others.

You will realize that the _need_ to be liked is a weakness and that it doesn't serve you.

When you try to _sell_ yourself, you will _ALWAYS_ sell yourself short.

Do the work!

Keep your head down and pay attention to your surroundings but don't be distracted by them. Your vision is clear, Dreamer and your time will come.

Be patient.

Keep the faith.

KEEP GOING!!!

105
WHAT ARE YOU SO AFRAID OF?

Dearest Dreamer,

For the first time in a long time, I sat with my fear today.

I explored why I was afraid and how that fear has been holding me back.

My fear of failure, coupled with imposter syndrome, led to a few anxiety attacks while I was writing these letters.

I decided to lean into the fear and right now, I am six letters away from completing this first volume.

Without GOD, none of this would be possible.

Fear kept me from writing and it kept me from sharing my writing with others, until now.

Do not let fear keep you from pursuing your promise and walking in your purpose!

Stand in your power.

Your creativity is your power.

Share your gifts.

Do the thing that you are afraid to do.

There is a blessing in facing your fears.

You will know hardship and struggle throughout this journey but don't let that stop you.

The act of *being* afraid is worse than the experience of *feeling* fear.

In order to overcome the former, you must first overcome the latter.

In other words, you must take <u>action</u>.

<u>*The more action you take, the less fear you will feel over time.*</u>

Understand that it is always worse in your mind than it is in reality.

Sure, the journey is not all sunshine and rainbows but would you appreciate the warmth of the sun or the brilliance of the rainbow if you had not come through the storm first?

Push through the fear.

<u>You will make it to the other side.</u>

Your promise is waiting.

You may come out of it with a few bumps and bruises but don't let that stop you.

KEEP GOING!!!

106

BELIEVE ME AND I WILL SHOW YOU

Dearest Dreamer,

I heard a saying once that goes,

"Man says, show me and I will believe you. GOD says, believe me and I will show you."

If you are reading this, Dreamer, then I overcame my fear and decided to believe in GOD, finishing the first volume of letters and releasing them into the world.

GOD used this opportunity to show me that GOD's grace is, in fact, sufficient and made perfect in my weakness.

In order to complete this task and push past the fear, I had to rely on something greater than myself.

Believe in your promise, Dreamer.

Believe that you will overcome any obstacle and make it to the other side of your struggle.

<u>Believe that your struggle is working for your good.</u>

Believe that you will be shown and made a believer in the power of GOD's grace.

KEEP GOING!!!

107
NONE BUT OURSELVES

Dearest Dreamer,

Have you ever heard Bob Marley's *Redemption Song*?

If you haven't heard it, do yourself a favor and go listen to it.

The lyrics are so powerful.

"Emancipate yourself from mental slavery; none but ourselves can free our mind. Have no fear for atomic energy for none of them can stop the time..."

He goes on to say,

"How long shall they kill our prophets while we stand aside and look? Some say it's just a part of it; we've got to fulfill the book."

The lyrics remind me that it is all a game, Dreamer.

It is the game of LIFE.

Be careful not to get caught up in it.

Know that you are covered and divinely protected.

Know that no one is coming to save humanity.

We must save ourselves.

We save ourselves by doing the work and healing the wounds from our painful experiences and past struggles.

On an individual level, we must all do the work.

Collectively, we must live the work we have done on the individual level.

Understand that we are the majority and not the minority.

Open your eyes, Dreamer.

Now is your time.

It is **OUR** time!

Awaken.

Expand.

Explore.

Act.

Believe.

In this moment of awakening, let us write our own *Redemption Song*.

Let us turn the tide and create opportunities for future generations to thrive.

Start developing that idea, Dreamer.

Start that company.

Start that non-profit.

Change the world.

Impact the people around you.

One small act at a time.

One person at a time.

Be a light.

KEEP GOING!!!

108

THE PATIENCE TO BECOME

DEAREST DREAMER,

I saw a quote while watching a YouTube short about something Michael Jordan once said.

"You're afraid of what I could become. I'm afraid of what I won't become. I have something that is more important than courage; I have patience. I will become what I know I am." (Michael Jordan)

Patience is the difference between becoming or not.

Be patient, Dreamer.

You may think you are ready now and in some ways, you may be, but be patient anyway and know that your time is coming.

You will become what you know you are.

KEEP GOING!!!

109
LOUD CHIPS

Dearest Dreamer,

Stasha and I were sitting on the couch watching something on Netflix recently.

I was eating chips and the crunching sound seemed obnoxiously loud in my head.

I apologized to Stasha for making noise and crunching on chips while we were watching a movie.

"The chips are always louder in your head," she told me.

The phrase was simple but it struck me and ultimately inspired this letter.

You are working hard, Dreamer.

You are building in silence and keeping your head down.

<u>Whatever you do, do it for the love of creating something and expressing yourself.</u>

Do it because you love it.

Do not do it for a reaction from others.

Do it to validate yourself and bring your ideas to life.

The criticism is always louder in your head.

The negativity is always louder in your head.

The fear is always louder in your head.

Share your gifts.

Shine your light.

Enjoy the experience of engaging in creative self-expression.

Do not let anyone or anything stop you on your mission.

Remain on your path and have faith that your time will come.

KEEP GOING!!!

110

HARD TIMES

Dearest Dreamer,

You are going through a hard time right now.

Things have fallen apart.

You do not appreciate the hard times yet, but one day you will.

Understand that these moments are meant to strengthen you, not destroy you.

Hard times are stepping stones towards your heart's desires.

They are a part of the process that prepares you to reach your desired result, giving you the fortitude and wisdom to sustain your future success.

Your challenges are blessings.

Your reward for overcoming your last challenge, is your next challenge.

You are still here, which means that you have a one hundred percent success rate for overcoming obstacles and challenges.

Whatever the setback, you survived it.

You are an overcomer.

Apply what you have learned in the process and **KEEP GOING!!!**

111
THANK YOU!

MOST HIGH GOD,

Thank you!

For my family.

For my gifts.

For my friends.

Thank you.

For every way made and roadblock removed.

For every enemy who taught me to love myself and every friend who taught me the same.

Thank you.

For a new day and an opportunity to right my wrongs.

For this collection of letters and the experiences that inspired them.

For this opportunity to share my gifts.

Thank you.

For every *"no"* that led to a *"yes."*

For every time I was rejected, I know now that I was being protected.

Thank you.

For carrying me every time I wanted to give up.

Thank you.

For being that still, small voice in my heart that has guided me along the way.

I know you are *REAL*.

Thank you.

For the journey and the version of myself that the journey helped to produce.

Thank you.

For Your love.

For strength.

For guidance.

For protection.

For peace.

For joy.

Thank you.

For the *strength, courage* and *faith* to **KEEP GOING!!!**

AUTHOR'S BIO

Shawn L. Bagley Jr. is a writer, creative and entrepreneur. Shawn's entrepreneurial journey began at the age of 22 when he took a leap of faith and started his first consulting firm. Specializing in business development and strategic planning, he worked diligently until he faced a significant setback at 26, losing everything and being forced to start over.

This experience turned out to be a blessing in disguise, marking a crucial turning point in his life that led to self-discovery and personal growth.

In 2019, Shawn launched his second consulting firm, BluLight Consulting LLC. Over the past decade, he has honed a unique set of skills that he uses to inspire others, foster collaboration, and assist clients in framing their strategies to bring their visions to life.

linkedin.com/in/sjb-the-alchemist
youtube.com/@BluLightConsultingLLC